Latin Americans with Palestinian Roots

Viola Raheb

First Edition

Latin Americans with Palestinian Roots
Viola Raheb

———————

Copy right © 2012 Diyar Publisher

ISBN -13 : 978-1478389613
ISBN -10 : 1478389613

Art direction : Diyar Publisher
Designer : Engred Anwar Al-Khoury
Printing press: Latin Patriarchate

———————

Supported by :
Consolidated Contractors Company

Cover picture provided by PalestineRemembered.com

1. Palestinian - Latin America - History 2. Palestinian - Emigration and Immigration 3. Palestinian Christian - History - 20th Century. I. Title

F1419.P35R33 2012

w w w . d i y a r . p s

Contents

Forward

This study is part of a bigger initiative of Diyar Consortium and is under the "Palestinian Christians: Strengthening Identity, Activating Potential" programme. The aim of the programme is to encourage and enable Palestinian Christians to engage more fully in Palestinian society at large, thereby strengthening the social fabric of Palestinian society as a whole, actively maintaining the Christian witness in Palestine, and stemming the outward flow of Palestinians from their ancestral lands. The initiative consists of four parts:

1. A mapping exercise designed to identify and study Palestinian Christian churches, church-related organisations (CROs), and Christian communities and individuals, as well as their needs and resources.
2. The development, through consultation with church, CRO and community leaders, as well as the community at large (especially those not currently involved in church/CRO activity), of a shared, comprehensive, ecumenical strategic vision for Christian engagement in Palestine.
3. The implementation of this strategy, both individually as well as in cooperation with others, through a variety of activities that would prepare and cultivate young leaders within the Christian community.
4. The documentation of the activities of the initiative, in writing and in audio-visual productions, as well as providing background information on the history of Palestinian Christians.

In 2008, Diyar published its first book "Palestinian Christians - Facts, Figures and Trends", which mapped Palestinian Christian presence in Palestine. This second book in this series aims at mapping the Latin American community with Palestinian roots, with special focus on Honduras, El Salvador, Nicaragua, Guatemala, Costa Rica, and Chile. It is our hope that through this publication the networking capacity of the Palestinian Christian community will expand to include their sisters and brothers in Latin America. Soon, Diyar will release a third book by Johnny Mansour mapping the Palestinian Christian community within the Green Line (Israel).

I would like to thank all the authors for participating in this book project and for their valuable time, energy, and thought-provoking articles. My sincere thanks go to Viola Raheb for coordinating this project. Special thanks go to Ms. Arda Aghazarian for doing a great job in editing this book and to Ms. Engred Khoury for the design. Special thanks go to the Consolidated Contractors Company (CCC) for funding the publication of this book, thus making it available in print for a wider audience.

Rev. Dr. Mitri Raheb
President, Diyar

Sisters and Brothers in the Diaspora: Palestinian Christians in Latin America

Viola Raheb

Why Latin and Central America

Palestinian immigration to Latin and Central America is considered one of the earliest in the modern history of the Palestinian people. Already in the mid-nineteenth and early twentieth century, Palestinians started to immigrate to Latin America. The Palestinian immigration to Latin America is seen as being composed of three waves: the first under the Ottoman Empire (1860-1916), the second under the British Mandate (1918-1948), and the third after the Nakba (1948). At the same time, it is important to note that during the second Intifada and between the years 2000-2005 another wave of Palestinian Christian immigration to Latin America took place, though not major in its number. The majority of the immigrants from the first wave were identified by the travel documents they were carrying and were considered, and are still to some extent, as Turks or as Syrians. According to the various researches done, the percentage of Christians among the total Palestinian immigrants to Latin America is being estimated at almost 80-85%. Due to the complexity of registration at the time of arrival, it is very difficult to have accurate numbers of Palestinian descendants in Latin America. Nevertheless, some scholars estimate the number at around half a million; the highest number of Palestinian immigrants being in Chile, while the highest percentage is considered to be in Honduras, where Palestinians make up almost 3% of the population. Today, Latin America has the biggest Palestinian Diaspora community outside the Arab World. At the same time, and taking into consideration the fact that the majority of this Diaspora community is of Christian Palestinian background, it also stands for the biggest Christian Palestinian community in the world, even in comparison to the original homeland.

The various studies show that these immigrants were able to develop a very solid economic ground and were able to become a major player within the economic sector of their new country of residence. At the same time, many of the second and third generation of these immigrants were able to develop influence within the media and the political arena. Nevertheless, the knowledge about these communities is very little even among Christian Palestinians themselves, and, accordingly, networking and exchange are week. This study comes to shed some light on the Palestinian Christian Diaspora in Latin America and is a first effort in trying to map the biggest Christian Palestinian community in the Diaspora.[1]

Latin and South America, a Source of Hope for Palestine

The political and economic developments in Latin America at the beginning of the twenty-first century and the rise of its role in regional and global politics have drawn a lot of international attention. Recently, Latin America has become a major source of hope for Palestinians. The ongoing wave of political developments in Latin America in connection with the Palestinian question has led to the recognition of an independent Palestinian state by many Latin and South American countries. Brazil, Argentina, Bolivia, Chile, Ecuador, Peru, Guyana, Paraguay, Uruguay, and Suriname all recognized an independent Palestinian state between December 2010 and February 2011. Yet, several Latin American countries, including Cuba, Venezuela, Nicaragua, and Costa Rica, had already either made a symbolic recognition of the Palestinian state or recognized a Palestinian state prior to this wave. The stand of Latin American countries at the UN General Assembly in relation to the Palestinian bid for statehood, and its vote in the UNESCO for a full membership of Palestine in the UN agency brought this recognition into a new political level. The political stand of these Latin American countries is fostering the hope among the Palestinian political leadership and the Palestinians in general. Yet, in spite of this political euphoria, especially among the Palestinians, the presence of the Palestinian Diaspora community in Latin America and their possible role in contributing to these developments is almost absent from the discussion. Is there a role this community is playing? What possible role could it play in terms of relating to Palestine and the political developments? In recent years more importance has been given to studying the role of Diaspora communities in peace efforts and peace initiatives. In March 2011, the United Nations Meeting of Civil Society in Support of Israeli-Palestinian Peace met in Montevideo, Uruguay, under the theme "Engaging civil society in Latin America and the Caribbean for peace and reconciliation between Israelis and Palestinians." The conference also addressed the possible role of the Palestinian and Jewish communities in Latin America in regard to fostering peace endeavors, as they have a long history of coexistence in Latin America.

Multiple Identities

In the course of preparing for this book, I had to contact several individuals and organizations in Latin and Central America, which was a challenging experience beyond the issue of language borders. One of the fascinating experiences was the reaction of persons with an Arab or a Palestinian background. Almost all of them were people of the fourth or fifth generation of immigrants to Latin and Central America. All of them, without any exception, referred to their Arab or Palestinian roots. This reference varied from one to another. While some said that they do not know exactly where their family came from (they assumed the origin to be Palestine, Syria, or Lebanon), others could name the exact place (country and town) of origin of their families. There were also some who introduced themselves as Christian Palestinians from Chile, Mexico or whatever Latin American country they were citizens of.

Almost all of them have never been to Palestine or to any other Arab country, and they do not speak or understand the Arabic language. While understanding themselves as Latinos, they feel at the same time the Arab and Palestinian roots that are a part of their identity. Roberto Marin Guzman writes in his paper, "In Central America, the second, the third, and in certain cases even the fourth generation of Palestinian descendants have lost the Arabic language. They still have a clear desire to defend the Palestinian people and to rescue the Arab cultural values and traditions."[2] Nicole Saffie Guevara and Lorenzo Agar Corbinos write: "Although the descendants consider themselves Chileans, the first, second, third, and even fourth generations born in the country somehow still identify themselves as Arabs."[3] Prof. Monzar Frohoor also addresses this point: "Even today, although Palestinian descendants born in Central America identify themselves as citizens of these countries, most of them refer to Palestine as their roots."[4] These observations among generations of Palestinian descendants could be seen as indicators of a rather positive identity formation process that recognizes the differences between the cultural traditions of their forefathers and foremothers and that of their new homeland and such allows multiple identities to exist. It is this multiple identity that is challenging the assumption that due to being assimilated in their communities, descendents of Palestinians in Latin America choose not to identify themselves as Palestinians.

Christian Palestinians in Publications

n the recent decades, the scholar interest in addressing the Arab immigrant communities and their history in Latin and South America has increased immensely. Many books and researches[5] have been written on the Arab immigrants in general while others addressed particularly the Palestinian immigration to Latin and South America. Some universities[6] have even developed new research projects that are addressing the issue of Middle Eastern immigration to Latin America. However, looking at the studies and publications shows that Palestinian Christians played only a marginal role in the content of the studies. The religious affiliation of the Palestinian immigrants is not at the heart of the research, rather it comes as statistical background when describing the Palestinian community in this region. Only very few addressed the Christian Palestinian community as such. Among them are the studies of Prof. Nancie L. Gonzalez ("The Christian Palestinians of Honduras: An Uneasy Accommodation"),[7] Olivier Prud'homme ("Los Cristianos de la region de Euphrata (Palestina) y sus practicas comerciales en el Salvador entre 1886 y 1918"),[8] and the MA thesis of Rosa Araya Suazo from Chile ("La iglesia ortodoxa en chile. patriarcado de antioquia y todo el oriente").[9] One could think that the religious affiliation of the migrant communities is not a point of interest for scholars, which is definitely not accurate since many studies do address this point specifically. Various studies have been made on the Muslim[10] and Jewish[11] communities. At the same time, there is more and more scholarly interest in addressing the factor of religion in identity formation with regard to migration and diaspora. To what extent does the migration process change religious traditions and practices? How does religion influence the process of migration and social integration for assimilation?[12]

The role of Religion within the Palestinian Diaspora in Latin America

The issue of religion and religious affiliation played a role in the immigration of people from the Ottoman state to the Americas already at its outset. Entering into the new country brought a religious mobility with it. In his work on Ottoman emigration to America, 1860-1914, Kemal Karpat writes that even Muslim immigrants from the Ottoman state chose to enter as "Syrians" or "Christians" in order to not jeopardize their entry. "Many took on Christian names, and it is certain that a large number actually converted to Christianity (or their children did)."[13]

While the aspects of ethnicity and culture have been discussed in addressing the Palestinian Diaspora in Latin America, the aspect of religion has been almost absent in addressing the role of religion in the experience of the Christian Palestinian Diaspora in Latin America. What role did religion take in the self-understanding of the Palestinian Diaspora community in Latin America? Was it just one component of their identity, or did it play a significant role in developing their new diasporic identity? How did their Christian religious identity develop in the new country? How did the religious mobility influence their identity?

Looking historically at the denominational character of the Palestinian Christians, who emigrated from Palestine in the nineteenth century, shows that they were of various Christian religious affiliations. The fact that the majority of the Christian Palestinian immigrants belonged to the Greek Orthodox Church is a reflection of the denominational affiliation within Palestine itself, where the Greek Orthodox Church is the biggest among the local Churches.

There have been changes within this Christian religious affiliation of Palestinian Christian immigrants to Latin America due to various reasons. There has been mobility within the affiliation to the Eastern Orthodox Church itself. The majority of the Palestinian Christian Orthodox in Latin America today belongs to the Orthodox Church of Antioch, which is not the same as the Orthodox Church in Palestine, namely the Greek Orthodox. Researching the web of the Orthodox Church in Chile[14] shows that already as early as 1916 priests of Palestinian origin were ordained to serve the local Christian Palestinian Orthodox community. Among the names listed in their chronology of priests serving the Orthodox Church are the names of Father Juri Solomon, Father Nicholas Touma, and Father Constantin Ziade, all three originally from Beit Jala. At the same time, there is mobility among Palestinian Christian Orthodox descendants toward the Russian Orthodox Church in Latin America.

The records show that there is also a religious mobility toward the Roman Catholic Church, either as a sign of adaption to the new context or as a result of the intermarriage between descendants of Palestinian Christians with the local community. This mobility toward the Roman Catholic Church is clearly seen in terms of comparing the religious affiliation of the various generations, as stated by Nicole Saffie Guevara and Lorenzo Agar Corbinos.[15] Some Palestinian Christians also got married to members of the indigenous communities within the new countries and, accordingly, came in contact with indigenous religions.

At the same time, there is also mobility toward other Christian religious denominations within the new countries, such as the Evangelical Churches. Some Evangelical Churches, like the Baptist Church, developed new ministries especially for Arabs. The Arabic Evangelical Church of São Paulo, Brazil, for example, was established as early as 1954.

Nevertheless, it is important to note that this religious mobility of Palestinian Christians varied from one host country to the other, as did the religious constellation of the communities from one country to the other.

At the same time, the role of other Arab Christian communities in the formation of the new religious affiliation among Palestinian Christians has also played an important role. For instance, Syrian and Lebanese Christian communities within the new countries served as social and religious networks for Palestinian Christians in Latin America. This also had an impact on the religious mobility.

Some descendants of Christian Palestinians describe a kind of hybridization in terms of their religious belonging. Their religious identity today includes elements of various traditions both from the religious traditions of their ancestors as well as from the new acquired religious traditions. In his paper, Roberto Marin Guzman comments on this issue: "The ornaments of wooden saints and icons, following the traditional forms of Middle Eastern Orthodox Christians, are combined with some Mayan Indian decorations."[16]

In some of the researches[17] on the Palestinian Diaspora in Latin America, scholars underline the integration, some even the assimilation, of Palestinian Christians within the new country. For some, the religious affiliation is a positive contributing factor for their successful integration and assimilation. This observation seems to be very appealing when looked at from current perspective.

However, reading the papers in this book show also the difficulties and hardships encountered by the first immigrants.

Christian Palestinians in Palestine and the Palestinian Christians Diaspora in Latin America

The study "Palestinian Christians: Facts, Figures and Trends - 2008" estimates the number of Palestinian Christians in the West Bank, Gaza Strip, and Jerusalem at 51,710, which makes 1.37 percent of the Palestinian population.[18] The majority of Palestinian Christians live today outside of Palestine. This ongoing immigration of Palestinian Christians has very much influenced both the Churches and the society. In the book "Christian Presence in the Holy Land," Fu'ad Farah states that the effect of this immigration varied from one Church to another. According to his data, the Armenian Orthodox Church was the one to suffer most from immigration, having lost almost 61 percent of its members, followed by the Assyrian Orthodox Church with almost 50 percent, the Arab Greek Orthodox Church with 32 percent, the Roman Catholic Church with 28 percent, the Greek Catholic with 15 percent, and the Protestant Churches with 8 percent.[19]

Family networks in the Diaspora have functioned as a generator for new migration among family members, a phenomena that can also be traced through researching the family names of Palestinian immigrants to Latin America, as Roberto Marín-Guzmán has shown.[20] Today many of these family names are no longer present in Palestine and can only be found in the Diaspora, as stated in the work of Dr. Musallam.

The future of the Christian Palestinian community is very much related to the issue of connecting to our faithful living in the Diaspora. Developing a sense of community and solidarity with our sisters and brothers who at a certain stage had to leave our homeland is essential for strengthening our understanding of who we are and who we want to be. Efforts are needed from the local churches and their CROs to link between all Palestinian Christians, those who still live in Palestine and those who are in the Diaspora.

It is our hope that this book is a first step for the dwindling Christian Palestinian community in Palestine to rediscover and reconnect with their sisters and brothers in the Diaspora.

The Formative Stages of Palestinian Arab Immigration to Latin America and Immigrants' Quest for Return and for Palestinian Citizenship in the Early 1920's

Adnan A. Musallam

Early Immigration from the Ottoman State to the Americas

The Mediterranean region witnessed in the last quarter of the nineteenth century waves of emigration from the Ottoman State. Nevertheless, emigration to the Americas was an inseparable part of international migration of human waves, which started between 1880 and 1920 from South and Central Europe and from the Ottoman Empire to the United States. Their number was estimated at 25,000,000: Italians, Greeks, Slavs, Jews, Ottomans, and others. The number of Arab Ottomans from Greater Syria (now Lebanon, Palestine, Syria, and Jordan) in this immigration was estimated to be 250,000 persons, not to mention the thousands of emigrants who ventured to Latin America.[21]

According to a report by the Ottoman Consul in the City of Buenos Aires in Argentina, 46,000 Ottoman immigrants arrived between 1911 and 1913. The Consul urged his government to put an end to this phenomenon.[22] The number of Ottoman immigrants to the Americas between 1860 and 1914 was estimated at 1,200,000 including 33,000 who came from Syria.[23]

The major factors that attracted immigrants to the Americas were economic. The tremendous industrialization which was taking place in the United States required manpower; this was guaranteed by the large number of immigrants. High wages and rumors that the American government was distributing agricultural land free of charge to anyone who migrated to the western parts of the United States (Homestead Act 1862) gave immigrants additional incentives.[24]

The Ottoman Foreign Ministry, furthermore, received many applications submitted by Brazilian landowner Paolo Duval from Sao Paulo asking for large numbers of Ottoman agricultural workers.[25] News about fortunes made by pioneers of emigration and checks sent to the mother country motivated others to follow suit. In 1914, emigrants from geographical Syria sent home remittances estimated at 8,000,000 dollars.[26]

It is worth mentioning that areas where early immigrants had settled became an attractive factor for other family members and relatives who subsequently immigrated, not for economic reasons but to join relatives. Between 1908 and 1909 family relations were the main reason for 95% of Syrian immigration to the United States.[27] This factor played a considerable role in the firm establishment and continuity of emigration that exists today.

Early Emigration from Ottoman Palestine

Historically, Palestine was connected in all aspects of life with Ottoman Greater Syria since 1516. Artificial boundaries which now separate the Palestinian from the Syrian, the Syrian from the Lebanese, and the Jordanian from the Palestinian took shape in the wake of the French and British agreements as embodied in the Sykes-Picot Agreement (May 1916), the military occupation system, the Anglo-French Agreement (September 1918), the decisions of San Remo (April 1920), and the Cairo Conference (March 1921).[28]

Emigration from Palestine, thus, was an integral part of this movement from Ottoman Greater Syria. The fundamental motivating factor for emigration was the deteriorating economic and political condition in the Holy Land, which left its mark on all population sectors. Outside influences escalated with the opening up of Palestine and Syria to new Western influences and technological innovations. As a result of the Industrial Revolution in Europe and the accompanying colonial movements in the Arab World, the region entered the Western economic network. Thus, "it was useless for local hand-made products to compete with European mass produced goods, severely affecting the local economy and deepening the political and economic servitude to the European system."[29]

Instability in the region, furthermore, played a significant role in escalating emigration. The years between 1792 and 1853 were characterized by feudal disorders, wars, economic paralysis, and demographic deterioration in the Ottoman Empire. Bribery, favoritism, and administrative corruption were widespread. Peasants who constituted the great majority of the population felt the pinch of taxes and levies. Thefts spread everywhere. The word "Khawa", a levy imposed on the weak by the strong, became an integral part of people's daily dictionary. In addition, the continual wars of the Ottoman State in the nineteenth century and the beginning of the twentieth century drained the number of youths as emigration became an exit and a means for youths to dodge the draft and escape armed conflicts including that of the First World War (1914 – 1918).[30]

In addition to the above-mentioned factors, we should mention that the existence of the Holy Places in Palestine, the importance of Jerusalem and Palestine in the international arena, the spread of foreign religious institutions in the Holy Land, and the crowds of visitors and pilgrims that came to Palestine from all over the world (mixing with Christian Arab interpreters and sellers of memorial curios who knew many foreign languages) eventually led to an increase in the awareness in Europe and the New World of Palestinian Arabs. This increased their desire to see those countries and immigrate to them in order to exploit the available economic opportunities, as is the case with people all over the world.

Information available to us indicates that the emigration of the Palestinians started in the last quarter of the nineteenth century. However, the first death among the emigrants to Latin America, recorded in the registers of the Latin Parish priest's office in Bethlehem, goes back to 7 September 1796. The deceased emigrant's name was Andrea Francis Hanna Dawid from the Tarajmah Quarter in Bethlehem.[31] The question that arises: Was Dawid's presence in Latin America simply an isolated phenomenon, or was it part of a wider Palestinian presence in those lands? What was the nature of Dawid's journey? Are there any similar cases in the Parish's office or other registers? This data must be scrutinized comprehensively. However, at least it confirms that the Palestinians were "years ahead of Arab immigrants to explore the wilds of America," and that Palestinians preceded their Lebanese brethrens in emigrating to the New World, although on a smaller scale, and did not settle down in the countries they went to as the Lebanese did. This was confirmed by the elder of the Arab Lebanese community in Brazil in the 1950s, Rizq Allah Haddad, as mentioned in the book, "Arab Speakers in South America." According to him, two brothers from the family Zakhariya from the Tarajmah Quarter in Bethlehem were among the first Arabs who arrived in Brazil in 1874. They sold mother-of-pearl curios such as rosaries, crosses, and icons in the main jewelers' street in Rio.[32]

Furthermore, international exhibitions held in the United States played a pioneering role in attracting Palestinian merchants from Bethlehem. Many of them came to visit the Philadelphia Exhibition of 1876, the Chicago Exhibition of 1893, and the St. Louis Exhibition of 1904, carrying with them Holy Land products such as mother-of-pearl, olive wood, and Nabi (Prophet) Moses stone, so as to exhibit and sell them to the faithful.

According to oral traditions, Bethlehemites like Geries Ibrahim Suleiman Mansoor Handal, Geries Anton Abul-'Arraj, Hanna Khalil Morcos, and Mishel and Gabriel Dabdoub, and others attended these international exhibitions. The Handal brothers eventually settled down in New York while the Dabdoub brothers, who received a medal during the Chicago Exhibition, returned to their native town. It so happened that a Mexican merchant was impressed with the Bethlehem products in the Chicago International Exhibition that he and Hanna Khalil Morcos agreed that the latter would travel to Mexico with a number of Holy Land products. That is what Morcos did. He returned to Bethlehem, gathered various Bethlehem products, traveled to Mexico in 1895, and settled in that country. Others followed, such as Geries Anton Abul-'Arraj, who went with his wife Sarah Dawid to the Republic of Guatemala after the termination of the 1893 International Exhibition. Having made his fortune selling Holy Land products, he decided to stay in that country and eventually took up trade.[33]

As one Western observer wrote:

"Hundreds of them have emigrated, consigning themselves from Jaffa to a Marseilles steerages agent with no notion of their ultimate destination. They can be found peddling lace anywhere from Haiti to the Argentine. Out of an arm basket and a five-peso credit they create bank accounts and fine stores. They emigrate as peasants in a fez and skirt; ten years later they show up in Bethlehem in a hat and trousers, and their former neighbors... in fezzes and skirts... address them as effendi."[34]

The news of these pioneers, their newly found wealth, and the cheques they sent to their relatives to erect spacious homes like those of Jacir, Handal, and Hermas, to mention only a few, spread far and wide. This created jealousy in the hearts of others. Some Syrians and Lebanese followed the example of their Palestinian brethren in selling Holy Land curios until the number of professionals increased and rumors spread that these products were manufactured in Europe. Thereafter, Westerners abstained from buying curios. Inevitably Palestinian merchants had to turn elsewhere; settlement and free trade consequently began. Initially, roaming peddlers followed the example of their Lebanese and Syrian brethren and penetrated Central and South America. They chose Chile, Peru, Bolivia, Colombia, and Honduras. In time, Chile became a main center for immigrants from the sister towns of Bethlehem and Beit Jala. The first Palestinian immigrant to enter Chile was the late Jubra'il D'eiq from the Tarajmah Quarter in Bethlehem. That was in 1880. He was followed by the late Yusuf Jacir from Bethlehem and the late Yusuf Geries Salah from Jerusalem. The three of them worked together in commerce.[35] However, according to the Palestinian Ambassador to Chile, Dr. May Kaileh, "The first Palestinian registered in the official registries of Chile was in 1840 in the fifth region, i.e., in Vina del Mar."[36] It appears that the history of Bethlehem and Palestinian emigration to Latin America needs to be reexamined in light of this new piece of information from Chile and from Bethlehem concerning Andrea Francis Hanna Dawid.

In the beginning, emigration was slow and temporary as the fundamental aim was making a fortune and returning home. However, between 1908 and 1918, coups, wars, and compulsory military service resulted in a notable rise in the number of emigrants. With the outbreak of the First World War, the prices of basic goods went up sharply resulting in many shortages. In 1915 and 1916, hundreds of thousands of people were on the verge of death and starvation due to the spread of the typhus epidemic. Collective fleeing from the draft became a familiar phenomenon. Thus, the slow and temporary emigration was transformed gradually into a dangerous social phenomenon in whose bitter reality Bethlehem and Palestine continue to experience.

Emigration from Bethlehem and Palestine in the British Era, 1917-1948: Its Impact Locally and on the Diaspora

Emigration continued throughout the British Mandate in light of the deterioration of the country's political situation. Most emigrants made their way to Latin America. Large groups of emigrants followed each other, encouraged by relatives already living in Chile, Colombia, Peru, Honduras, and El Salvador. Very few emigrants arrived at the North American shores at this stage because American laws, enacted between 1917 and 1924, limited the immigration of non-Anglo-Saxons such as Italians, Slavs, Arabs, Asians, and Africans. They aimed at the preservation of the cultural and ethnic hegemony of the Anglo-Saxon whites. These same years witnessed the appearance of racist movements antagonistic to anyone who was Catholic, immigrant, foreigner, black, or Jew. One such movement was the Ku Klux Klan, which reached its climax in 1923 when its followers were estimated to be in the millions.[37]

Lack of official statistics makes it difficult to estimate the total number of Palestinian emigrants in this period, but the estimate of emigrants in 1936 was 40,000.[38] With the arrival of vast numbers of emigrants to main immigration centers in Latin America, certain streets in principal Latin American cities began to acquire Palestinian characteristics. At the same time the names of certain large families in Palestinian cities began to disappear gradually from local registers, resulting from collective emigration and family reunification in the Diaspora. Such was the case in Bethlehem with the following families (mentioned as samples only):[39]

Farahiyah Quarter	Anatra Quarter	Tarajmah Quarter	'Najaj rah Quarter	Hreizat Quarter	Qawawsah Quarter
Jada'	Shahin	Kamandari	al-'Alul	Abu Jarur	Abu Nifhar
D'eis	Dhawabah	Abu Fheilah	Qarqur	Hreizi	Sirriyeh
Barakah	Abu Gheith	Talamas	Hilwah	Abu Hermas	Abu Shunnar
Jidi	Silhi	Sam'an	al-Qabas	'Afanah	Bsiseh
Bkhit	Wardah	Tarud	'Duzman	Sahuriyah	Nquli
Dakkarat	Shamali	Dahburah	Za'nun	Dguban	
Miladeh		'Abis	Abu Arab	Adawi	
Zaitun			al-Chat'ah	al-Tqu'i	
Dardahiyyah				al-Bahri	
Silsik				Hasluf	
Shhadeh				Sabbagh	
Abu Shaqrah					
Mua'allim					
Jacir					

Palestinian folk literature looked with much anger and disgust at the mass emigration of young people to the Americas:

> *No America! May the father of your friends be cursed... You have taught young people to knock at your doors*
> *No America! May the father of your people be cursed... Your great wealth has incited young people (to leave their homes)*[40]

The Question of the Return of the Immigrants from Latin America

It is worth mentioning that a considerable number of immigrants in Latin America desired to return to their country, because they did not emigrate for the love of emigration but for the improvement of their economic conditions or in an attempt to flee the horrors of continual wars. After the end of the First World War, many decided to practice their natural right of return to their birthplace. The British authorities, however, closed the doors in their faces at a time when the doors of Palestine were wide open to Jewish immigrants. The Palestinian Citizenship Law was ratified in 1925 with the main aim of facilitating the granting of Palestinian citizenship to Jews coming to Palestine, according to Item 7 of the Mandate Charter.[41]

Lauren E. Banko points out the following:

> *The process of 'inventing' Palestinian citizenship was unlike anything else Great-Britain had done in their colonial empire, especially because they had to take into account international treaties and regulations, Ottoman laws and the Balfour Declaration as it was included in the Mandate's charter. While Palestinian nationality and citizenship laws were a product of the British Government's legislative process, citizenship's legal validity came from international law - the Treaty of Lausanne's law of state succession and the Mandate itself as international document. The entire five-year process of inventing citizenship in the crucial early 1920's created an enormous amount of questions the British dealt with over the status, sovereignty and civic rights of subjects as apposed to nationals or citizens in a mandated territory. British notions of citizenship were imported into Palestine after approval by His Majesty's Government (HMG) in London.* [42]

The Covenant of the League of Nation's Article 22, which clarified the mandate system, was vague about the citizenship of former Ottoman subjects.[43] Lauren E. Banko adds that article 7, which focuses on acquisition of nationality by Jewish immigrants, does not mention Arab inhabitants of Palestine.[44] Furthermore, the British saw Arab inhabitants as Ottoman citizens during the military and civil administrations during the period the Allies were at war with Turkey.[45] The international recognition of Palestinian nationality became operative in light of the peace treaty (Treaty of Lausanne) between Turkey and the Allies on 24 July 1923.[46] Concerning Palestinians residing abroad, Article 34 of the Treaty clearly mentions that these persons had two years to apply for the Palestinian nationality.[47]

Excerpts of immigrants' quest for Palestinian citizenship and the many problems encountered in their host countries as a result of not having citizenship were reported, discussed, and documented in leading Palestinian newspapers, mainly Jaffa's Filastin (Palestine) and Jerusalem's al-Jami'ah al-'Arabiyyah (The Arab Union) between 1926 and 1933.[48]

The Committee for the Defense of Immigrants Rights to Palestinian Citizenship

The notables of the Bethlehem region took up the case, under the leadership of Khalil 'Issa Morcos from Bethlehem, 'Atallah Hanna al-Najjar from Beit Jala, and 'Issa al-Khury Basil Bandak from Bethlehem (owner of the newspaper "Sawt al-Sha'b" and later Mayor of Bethlehem and founder of "The Committee for the Defense of Emigrants Rights to the Palestinian Citizenship" in 1927). The Committee led the campaign against the oppressive British policy that allowed the incoming alien Jewish immigrants to obtain citizenship under the easiest conditions, while placing numerous obstacles in the face of native-born Palestinians who wanted to return to their country. The Committee launched an appeal to the British people in the form of a booklet on the question of the emigrants and the obstacles created by the British authorities to prevent Palestinians abroad from obtaining Palestinian citizenship. 'Issa al-Bandak, Mayor of Bethlehem (1934-1938), raised the question before "Lord Peel's Royal Commission" that came to Palestine in 1936 to investigate disturbances and rebellion in the country, and to recommend for the partitioning of Palestine in 1937. The Royal Commission recommended in its report the facilitation of measures of return for those emigrants with genuine intentions who kept a continual personal contact with Palestine.[49]

The Defense Committee demanded in its campaign that all Palestinian immigrants residing abroad should be considered, at their request, Palestinian citizens, and that all Palestinian emigrants who have returned to Palestine or have temporarily stayed away should obtain their right to Palestinian citizenship as soon as they submit official applications to the relevant departments. The Defense Committee demanded that orders must be circulated to all British government representatives throughout the Palestinian Diaspora to defend and protect the interests of all Palestinian Arabs until the government acknowledged their right to Palestinian citizenship. "The government should consider these applications indicative of the feelings of Palestinian Arab public opinion in the country and aboard..."[50]

Problems Faced by Palestinian Immigrants

Concerning Palestinian emigrants who left the country before 1920, Britain considered them Turks because they traveled with Ottoman passports during Ottoman Turkish rule. This British stance totally contradicted Item 34 of the Treaty of Lausanne which stipulated that citizenship must be given to those who were born in countries which were once parts of the Ottoman Empire within two years of the effective date of the Treaty - 6 August 1924 - but no later than 6 August 1926.[51] However, the Government of Palestine did not enact the Palestinian Citizenship Law and did not promulgate it in the official gazette until 16 September 1925. Thus, the government wasted more than half of the period as specified in the Treaty. In addition to this tragedy, the British Government failed to circulate the Law in the local papers, neither did the British representatives in the Americas circulate it in the press so that emigrants could be informed.[52]

The British Ambassador in the Mexican capital stated that the British Government "had not authorized him to spend three pounds to publish the mentioned Law. In October 1927, the British Mandatory Government issued a statement saying, "The Palestinian citizenship is given to the emigrants who left the country after 1920 or before this date, and returned to the country and resided six months in it." As for the emigrants who had left the country before 1920 and did not return and constituted ninety per cent of all emigrants abroad, they were considered by the British to be Turks, completely ignoring the fact that they were not "Turks: by race, nationalism, language, or emotion."[53] As a consequence of this British policy, only one hundred applications were approved of a total of 9,000 submitted by emigrants wanting to return to their mother country.[54]

The British Government, on its part, expressed its readiness to defend the interests of those who had acquired citizenship, but it refused to protect those who did not acquire it, that is, the overwhelming majority. It did not want to bear the responsibility of a great number whose sole aim was to benefit from British protection, though item 12 of the Mandate Charter stipulates that "the Mandated Power had the right, too, to extend the protection of its ambassadors and consuls to Palestinian subjects living abroad."[55] When a delegation from the Palestinian community living in El Salvador met the British Consul and asked him to carry out this item, the Consul's reply was: "The British State accepted the mandate over the land of Palestine only, and this mandate does not include the affairs of the Palestinians."[56]

Palestinian emigrants deprived of their citizenship faced extremely difficult circumstances. For example, in July 1927 in El Salvador, the Government enacted a law forcing every merchant whose capital exceeded thirty pounds to register his name and produce his citizenship papers. If the merchant failed to observe this order, he would have his stores closed. When the Palestinians asked the British Consul to give them a citizenship certificate, he refused. When some Palestinians tried to obtain the Salvadorian citizenship to protect their interests, the government refused on the basis that their need to acquire citizenship did not stem from their love and commitment, but from personal benefit only.[57]

The immigrants who did not carry Latin American citizenship faced other difficulties:
- They could not travel from one country to another to tend commercial interests.
- The American republics, in particular El Salvador and Guatemala, enacted laws to deport anyone who did not possess citizenship.
- Coups and rebellions frequently happened in the American republics. Normally foreigners took shelter with their consuls; but Palestinians came under the mercy of the strong and thus became victims of blackmail.
- When immigrants were unable to obtain their citizenship, they were inevitably compelled to acquire the citizenship of the country in which they were residing, thereby gradually becoming out of touch with their country and relatives and losing the incentive of returning to found industrial and commercial projects. [58]

Settling Down in Latin America: Stories of Success and Failures

The Palestinian immigrants who did not acquire citizenship eventually settled in the Diaspora for good and played a pioneering role in the development of their new homes. Stories of the brilliant success of emigrants from Bethlehem and Beit Jala are numerous and documented. The following are examples: The Brothers Hunain and Nicola Jarur from the Hreizat Quarter in Bethlehem were extremely successful in the Chilean industries. This is evident in the economic projects they established, such as the Jarur Brothers' Factories of cotton goods employing about 3,000 laborers in an area of 80,000 square meters. Other examples are the Sahuri Brothers from Bethlehem who have erected a modem industrial city for cotton goods with an area of 150,000 square meters; the factories of Sulaiman Zummar from Beit Jala; the factories of Hermas Brothers from Bethlehem, and the factories of Abu Sabal Brothers from Beit Jala and hundreds others, all in Chile.[59]

Few are the stories we hear about emigrants who followed the example of the late 'Abdul Majid Shuman who traveled to the United States in 1911 carrying with him eight gold pounds. He returned home in 1929 to lay the foundation of the Arab Bank, which, since then, has become one of the greatest banking institutions in the Arab World.[60]

Little do we hear about such men as Badr and Ibrahim 'Abdullah al-A'ma (or Lama) who returned from Chile in 1927, armed with a knowledge of the art of photography and cinema. Their aim was to establish a cinema company in Palestine. However, a stop in Alexandria, Egypt, convinced them that opportunities in Egypt were better than in Palestine. They settled down and founded the Condor Cinema Film Company, which presented in May 1927, "A Kiss in the Desert", the first silent Arabic film in the history of Egyptian cinema. In the thirties and forties, Lama Studios became one of the major cinema companies in Egypt.[61]

Though success stories of immigrants are documented and available, thousands of stories of failures are not, such as the stories of those who could not return home despite their deep love, as they did not possess even the fare to return to their homeland. They preferred the hardships of life and a slow death in the Diaspora, as dignity would not allow them to return as failures and to become a joke to their fellow Palestinians back home.

Political Participation and Economic Success of the Palestinians of Christian Origin in Central America

Roberto Marín-Guzmán

Introduction

At the end of the nineteenth and early in the twentieth century, many Arabs emigrated to different countries in the world. The motives for these movements were diverse, ranging from economic, political, religious, to social reasons. To emigrate was undoubtedly a brave decision full of challenges. However, many hoped to find in another land the ways to improve their economic situation, practice their religion freely, or flee from political persecution in their own countries. Many others probably had great expectations for commercial activities that would glean great profits. These were the major reasons for many Arabs - mainly Palestinians, Lebanese, and Syrians - to leave their homelands and move to faraway countries in the last quarter of the nineteenth century and early in the twentieth. The purpose of this essay is to study the process of Palestinian immigration in the Central American republics. It will also analyze the different activities that the Palestinian immigrants of Christian origin and their descendants have engaged in these host countries, mainly their businesses, their industrial participation, and, finally, their financial strategies. The essay will also study their cultural contribution to the countries of Central America, as well as their political involvement as leaders in various administrative positions.

I will discuss the different periods of Palestinian immigration in Central America that presented diverse kinds of people to the region – people of different religions, social status, and cultural backgrounds – and this diversity certainly influenced their ultimate occupations in the five host countries, the traditional Central American republics. Undoubtedly, the majority of the first Palestinian immigrants at the turn of the century and during the first decades of the twentieth century were predominantly Christians of rural origin. They settled mainly in Honduras, El Salvador, Nicaragua, and Guatemala, with very few in Costa Rica. It is also important to point out that more recently, after the establishment of the State of Israel, and especially after the Six Days War of 1967, more Palestinians have arrived in Central America. In this more recent period of immigration, most of them are Muslims as opposed to those of Christian origin who characterized the previous emigration periods.

Palestinian immigrants of Christian origin have also had a political involvement in defence of the rights of the Palestinian people, and they have especially been active in Costa Rica and in Honduras. This essay will analyze these issues as well, and, finally, it will deal with the issue of assimilation of the Palestinian descendants into the societies of the host countries.

Through the various issues analyzed in this essay, one could obtain a major picture of the impact and political participation of the Palestinian immigrants of Christian background in the different nations of Central America.

Palestinian Immigration of Christian Origin in Central America: Analysis of Cases

The first Palestinian immigrants in Central America arrived in the late nineteenth century and early twentieth century when the Ottoman Empire still existed. Because of their arrival to Central America with Ottoman passports, many identified them as Turks. This still persists in the popular mind, which considers the Arab immigrants who arrived in this region with Ottoman documents as Turks. The same happened with many Lebanese and other Syrian Arab immigrants who reached Latin America during the Ottoman domination of the Arab Levant.

In the first period of immigration (from the last decades of the nineteenth century to the outbreak of World War I in 1914), the Palestinians of Christian faith settled in the different countries of the isthmus, with very few in Costa Rica. Many Palestinians started emigrating as early as the 1860s to different countries in the world with the intention of profiting from wood and mother-of-pearl craftsmanship.[62] In the 1890s, they started arriving to Central America because they had heard that in this region people would eagerly buy their handicrafts, as well as many other objects manufactured in the Holy Land. There are some oral traditions which indicate that many Palestinians of Christian origin first entered El Salvador. One oral tradition affirms that the first Palestinian who arrived to the isthmus, of whom neither his name nor his exact place of origin is provided, entered El Salvador by the port of Cutuco and left by the port of Acajutla, bound for another country in the area. The same has been confirmed by some of the descendants of Palestinian immigrants in San Pedro Sula, who stated that many of their ancestors stayed first in El Salvador before going over, by land, to Honduras.

In general terms, the Palestinians settled mainly in Honduras (where they arrived in large numbers,) then in El Salvador, Nicaragua, and, finally, in Guatemala during the first period of the immigration. Very few settled in Costa Rica. To this last country they arrived in larger numbers much later.[63] The following table of the number of Palestinian family names in Central America clearly illustrates this process:

Table No. 1:

Number of Palestinian last names found by travelers in Central America[64] (until 1955)

Country	Number of last names
Honduras	255
El Salvador	199
Nicaragua	25
Guatemala	23
Costa Rica	2
Total	504

Source: Nasri Salomón Jacir, Boletín de la Sociedad Caritativa de Belén, Commercial Press, Jerusalem, 1955-57, quoted by Nancie González, Dollar, Dove and Eagle. One Hundred Years of Palestinian Migration to Honduras, The University of Michigan Press, Ann Arbor, 1992, p.62, information extended and adapted by the author.

The Case of the Palestinians of Christian Origin in Honduras

The Palestinian immigrants of Christian origin in Honduras started arriving towards the end of the nineteenth century, the first case being recorded in 1899. After some isolated instances, the Palestinians, mainly from Bethlehem and the villages of Beit Sahur and Beit Jala (Ephrata region), arrived in Honduras in greater numbers and in a more systematic way, coinciding in 1906 with the Honduran government approval of a series of laws that were favorable for the immigrants. The period of the greatest Palestinian immigration to Honduras was from 1922 to 1931. Shortly afterwards, it declined due to the Depression of the 1930s, even though the immigration process to this country never completely stopped. Some Palestinians of Christian origin went to Honduras to visit relatives and to work for a period of time, hoping to return rich to Palestine.

Due to the 1929 Depression and parallel to these economic difficulties, several laws were approved in Honduras, in 1929 and 1934, tending to restrict the arrival of foreign immigrants, including the Palestinians. Those who arrived during the time these laws were in force had to pay extremely high prices for the right of immigration and many, as part of the new migratory policies, were forced to devote themselves to agriculture or to create new industries.[65] On the other hand, the British Mandate of Palestine encouraged the return of the Palestinian emigrants and restricted the exodus of many more. For this purpose the British authorities created new job opportunities, as is shown for those years by The Statistical Abstract of Palestine.[66] For the period of 1933-1934 there were in Honduras 592 Palestinians, the majority of Christian origin, documented as foreign residents. The number reached 812 in 1936-1937, to which clandestine immigration needs to be added.[67] Yet by the early 1930s, the Palestinian immigrants of Christian origin had already been very successful in commerce and in industry. As an example of their assimilation they even published their own weekly newspaper in Spanish, called El Eco de Palestina. In 1930, there were in Honduras 58 clothing factories, of which 20 belonged to Palestinian immigrants, among which La Perfección and La Sampedrana, both in San Pedro Sula, were the major ones.[68] La Perfección, for example, had 91 sewing machines, and gave jobs to 112 female workers in the textile industry. According to the statistics of the census, Palestinian immigrants of Christian origin controlled the major business in San Pedro Sula, El Progreso, Tela, La Ceiba, and other cities in 1931.[69]

The majority of these immigrants were Christians practicing Orthodox rites, even though some studies reveal that between 15 and 20 per cent of them were Muslim. Due to the paucity of records registering them as Muslim, it is possible to assume that they had either left silently without revealing their religion or that they converted to Christianity after their arrival in Central America;[70] as only 17 Muslim Palestinian families could be determined to be in Honduras. Undoubtedly, the Palestinian Muslims remain as a separate group from the other Palestinians, sharing with them neither family, nor places of origin, nor religion. It is likely that the number of Palestinian Muslims in Honduras has increased, but data are uncertain.

I will now turn to explain the ways Palestinian immigrants arrived in Honduras, the jobs and business opportunities that the country offered them, and their economic success mainly in the northern coast of the country. I will also analyze their political and cultural participation, as well as their assimilation to the Honduran society.

The northern coast of Honduras underwent enormous economic transformations from the 1870s onward mostly related to banana plantations. Because the country required a great number of services in this area, and due to its rapid development, this province attracted investors, producers, and merchants. Among them were the Palestinians, along with many other foreigners.[71] The Palestinians, mainly of Christian origin, started some commercial enterprises in this area. Very few of them cultivated bananas or worked for the banana companies on the plantations.[72]

In the first years after their arrival to the northern coast of Honduras at the beginning of the twentieth century, the Palestinians of Christian origin settled near the ports of La Lima, El Progreso, and Puerto Cortés, where there was great economic flux.[73] Because of this, the first Palestinian immigrants did not invest much money during these early times in big, luxurious, or comfortable houses, but rather lived in a very modest way. When traveling through rural areas to sell their products as itinerants, single men usually rented a room and, frequently, just a bed. These itinerant commerce practices were observed in 1928 by traveler Karl Sapper.[74] After marriage, the Palestinians usually obtained a house for their families, almost always above or behind their stores.

Although the Palestinian immigrants of Christian origin settled in many other towns and cities, San Pedro Sula has undoubtedly been one of the most important centers for their businesses.

They also lived in La Ceiba and Trujillo. They contributed from the beginning to the progress of the northern coast of Honduras. It is not clear if the city of San Pedro Sula grew so fast because of the work and businesses of the Palestinian immigrants, or if its growth had been the main attraction that led the Palestinian immigrants to settle in this city and its surrounding areas. The Palestinian immigrants also went to a great number of small towns, especially those along the railroad lines, where they took many products like food, clothes, and the necessary tools for banana production. Among the most important towns where they lived were: Santa Rita, Villa Nueva, Pimienta, San Manuel, El Porvenir, Olanchito, El Urraco, Chamelecón, Cofradía, and Choloma. The fact that they had settled in towns did not reduce their itinerant commercial activity, which they continued to practice, especially at long distance. At the beginning of the century, communication difficulties forced many Palestinians to walk great distances and then use canoes to reach certain places. They employed mules for other locations, and finally, also, trains where they existed. These transportation hardships made the products the Palestinians carried even more expensive, thus making the profits even greater.[75] In 1988 and still today there is evidence that some Palestinians practice itinerant commerce and carry certain products by automobile to other towns and cities. Frequently, they sold their products on credit to their customers.[76] After 1948, the Palestinians noticed that retuning to Palestine was even more uncertain than before. Since then, many who had not already done so, decided to invest massively and to settle permanently in Central America.

The Palestinian immigrants created, in a gradual process from 1900 to the present, a great number of businesses which generated new and important job opportunities for many people. For the period between 1900-1949 in the Department of Cortés, it was the Palestinians who, after the Hondurans of Spanish and other European descent, had the greatest number of businesses, which were bigger and more important than those of many other Central Americans.

In the Department of Cortés during the period 1900 to 1950, forty per cent of the investments came from Palestinian immigrants.[77] In the case of San Pedro Sula, between 1900 and 1986, Palestinian businessmen managed to reach seventy five per cent of the stores facing the six most important blocks in the commercial district. Furthermore, Palestinians own twenty seven per cent of the 900 stores located in the total San Pedro Sula commercial district. Likewise, they own fifty per cent of the existing hardware stores in the commercial district of this city. These data prove the prosperity of their economy. To all of this, one has to add that the Palestinians in these areas of Honduras were also buying land, especially during World War II. Since then, property values have risen rapidly.[78]

In their economic activities, the Palestinians in Honduras followed the tradition of forming family businesses, both in commerce and in industry. There are countless references to brothers or nephews moving to Honduras to join a business that an older brother or an uncle had started years earlier.[79] Some immigrants in Honduras returned to Palestine to find new assistants among their relatives. Others frequently went to find a wife, usually related through patrilineal ties, which explains why endogamy was common among Palestinian immigrants in Honduras in the early periods of immigration.[80]

Women have always been very active in economic occupations and were helping their husbands in the family businesses. In Palestinian businesses there has been a clearly recognizable tendency to seek partners, in the first place, among relatives. For the period between 1948-1988, calculations show this tendency in fifty one per cent of the cases. The partnership with other Arab non-relatives during the same period reached 10.6 per cent, while it reached 38.4 per cent with other non-Arabs.[81] Today in Honduras exists a very prosperous textile industry which belongs to the Palestinian Christian Kattan family. This factory is located in Choloma, in the Departamento de Cortés, and it offers new jobs and wealth to the country.[82] In the 1990s, the Kattan Group opened the free trade zone named Inhdelva, which by the year 2010 has attracted 30 companies. These companies rent 20 different buildings in Inhdelva from the Kattan Group. Inside this free trade zone, the Kattan Group has established six of its seven textile plants. These plants have been producing for well-known brands such as Van Heusen, Tommy Hilfiger, Arrow, Chaps, Izod, DKNY, Donald Trump, Oxford, Men's Warehouse, Hanes, Gildan, Gap, Ralph Lauren, Vanity Fair, Dickies, Nike, JC Penny, Best Uniforms, and Bass.[83] These textile plants have created 3,000 new jobs in the country, being therefore one of the major companies for the labor market in Honduras. In 2008-2009, this company was the major shirt-producer in Latin America.[84] The statistics for the year 2010 are not yet available.

Palestinians in Honduras live in a confluence of cultures. Many Palestinians, or their descendants, continue to build houses following traditional Middle Eastern customs, using flat roofs, and arched windows and doors. There are also a great number of typically Arab products for sale in the markets, such as cardamom, pistachios, figs, olives, grape leaves, sunflower seeds, etc. In visits to friends or relatives, the Palestinian forms of courtesy and hospitality are followed, mingled with those of Honduras. For example, in Honduras, to serve coffee at the beginning of a visit does not convey the message, as in Arab society, that the visitor must leave. It rather is a sign of Latin American tradition of hospitality. [85]

Palestinian descendants frequently play Middle Eastern music in their festivities, celebrations, weddings, baptisms, and birthdays. Usually there are also "belly dancers" at their parties. The cultural confluence is observed in that they often combine Arab music with other kinds of music in their celebrations. The ornaments of wooden saints and icons, following the traditional forms of Middle Eastern Orthodox Christians, are combined with some Mayan Indian decorations.

Palestinian immigrants in Honduras have founded several associations with the purpose of preserving some of their traditions and maintaining their unity. Among these organizations are those related to the Orthodox religion: the Orthodox Committee (Comité Ortodoxo), the Orthodox Ladies' Committee (Comité de Damas Ortodoxas), and the Juvenile Club (Club Juvenil).

The majority of the Palestinian immigrants in Honduras are Greek Orthodox and belong to the first Orthodox Church of Central America (founded in San Pedro Sula in 1963) which they consider the only purely Arab institution in Honduras.[86] This Church still maintains the same traditions as the Orthodox churches in the Middle East, such as the use of icons, hanging lamps, as well as other traditional decorations and religious practices indigenous to the Middle East. Amongst them, for example, is the use of the Julian calendar instead of the Gregorian. The Orthodox Church in Honduras has also had a distinguished political participation in the defense of the rights of the Palestinian people. It has collected large sums of money to help Palestinian refugees in the Middle East. The Church frequently holds masses for the martyrs of the Intifada (1987-1993 and 2000 to the present) and often buys complete pages in the local newspapers to advocate for the defense of the Palestinians. One influential name in this respect is Jorge Larach who, besides being a businessman who has invested in industry, also happens to be the owner of two of the major newspapers in Honduras, among them La Prensa, which has the largest circulation in Honduras.[87] La Prensa often publishes articles in defense of the rights of the Palestinians.

Among the other associations, there is the Palestinian Sports Club (Club Deportivo Palestino), the Honduran Feminine Arab Association (Asociación Femenina Hondureña Árabe) which is essentially a social group for chatting, listening to Arab music, and enjoying Arab dances, and the Honduran-Arab Cultural Center (Centro Cultural Hondureño Árabe) which has hosted recreational activities for the Palestinian families such as dances, picnics, and social gatherings. One of these centers also exists in Tegucigalpa.[88] Another association in which Palestinians also participated in is the Federation of American Arab Entities (FEARAB by its Spanish name, Federación de Entidades Americano-Árabe), which is made up of like-minded men regarding political views and actions. Many Hondurans believed back in the 1980s and 1990s that some of the members of FEARAB were fanatics and that they were even supporters of some of the factions of the PLO.[89]

The Bethlehemite Palestinians founded the Bethlehemite Association in Philadelphia in 1985 with the purpose of publishing information about the happenings in Bethlehem and in the Ephrata region in general. This association has also informed its members of the development of the Intifada, and gave updates about the deaths, births, and weddings of its members. Many Honduran-Palestinians belong to this association, and it will probably have a headquarter in San Pedro Sula with similar purposes in the near future.[90] The Palestinians of Christian origin have also organized an economic association called Investments Inc.

In general terms, Palestinian descendants in Honduras are integrated into the society of this country, as is proven by the participation of many of them in the most diverse fields including the professional, cultural, sports, etc. The economic area, however, is the one to which they have given their major contribution. It is important to point out that Palestinian descendants have not gone into the fields of law or to the academy, as demonstrated by Nancie González.[91] Some have participated actively in politics, such as Emin Abufele, a leader in the Partido Nacional, and Carlos Kattan who was a congressman representing the people of the Departamento de Cortés.[92] Carlos Flores-Facusse ran for the Presidency of the Republic twice, as candidate of the Partido Liberal, and was elected President of Honduras for the period 1998-2002.[93] Many others have reached important positions as officers of the Honduran army.[94]

Second and subsequent generations of Palestinians do not speak Arabic. They consider themselves Hondurans and are totally assimilated into this country. Some of them are Catholics, like the majority of Hondurans, even though the majority still practice the Orthodox religion. With that being said, many of the Palestinian descendants are interested in preserving Palestinian traditions and customs. Palestinians and their descendants in Honduras have also demonstrated an enormous and serious interest in the defense of the rights of the Palestinian people. This fervor is fed by information gathered first hand; that is to say, from new Palestinian immigrants who have arrived in recent years, especially after the rise of the second Intifada of 2000. Many immigrants have arrived recently to Honduras from the two Palestinian towns of Beit Sahur and Beit Jala, which have become real symbols of the Palestinian resistance.

The Case of the Palestinians of Christian Origin in El Salvador

The arrival of Palestinian immigrants in El Salvador, from the late nineteenth and early twentieth century, coincided with their immigration in Honduras. It is for this reason that many Palestinian families in El Salvador have relatives in Honduras, as is the case of the Handal, Siman, Salume, and other families.[95] The greatest Palestinian immigration period in El Salvador was from 1910 to 1925, with estimates on the number of Palestinian families being uncertain. An exact count is very difficult - some scholars believe it is impossible - since records frequently are scarce or non-existent.[96] Most of the Palestinian immigrants came from the area of Bethlehem as Orthodox Christians who had worked in agriculture for several generations. Some of them were also merchants before their exodus. Their arrival in El Salvador opened new economic opportunities for them and they rose on the social ladder quickly, taking advantage of the good opportunities and, undoubtedly, not without great personal effort.

The Palestinian immigrants in El Salvador settled all over the country, especially in San Salvador, San Miguel, Santa Ana, and La Unión. From the earliest times, they became merchants, and their major commerce was, above all, to sell clothing and footwear. The Handal family in La

Unión in the eastern part of the country developed other economic activities, mainly the exploitation of salt mines; a business they have kept up to the present day. Others, like the Khouri family, concentrated on agriculture, especially cotton, which they cultivated in the San Miguel area. They have also had great prosperity in this business. Other Palestinians have gone into the food business. The Safie family, for example, bought the baby food Gerber Industry, while the Salume, who arrived in El Salvador in 1914, have a super market chain. More recently they have devoted themselves to the wholesale business in an enterprise called Distribuidora Salume (Salume Distributing).[97] Some other Palestinian descendants have become so prosperous that they have been able to establish their own Shopping Centers, as the case of the Galerías Escalón of the Siman family.[98] Other Palestinian descendants have practiced diverse activities like the case of the Salume family, which has the leather tanning business and owns a great number of leather shops in El Salvador. Other members of the Salume family moved to Guatemala, where they have founded some instant coffee factories. 'Isa Miguel in El Salvador has had both domestic and international financial business, and nowadays he has also invested in Banco de la Vivienda (Housing Bank) in Guatemala.[99] As a consequence of their economic successes, Palestinian immigrants have been able to buy houses and other properties since the earliest times in the posh residential zone of La Flor Blanca. When this neighborhood became heavily commercial, Palestinian immigrants moved to other residential neighborhoods, like El Escalón, towards the mountains, because the city of San Salvador has extended in that direction.

Since early times, Palestinian immigrants and their descendants were interested in maintaining the group unity and preserving many of their traditions and customs. For this reason they founded the Club Palestino, (The Palestinian Club) later known as the Club El Prado. Despite repeated attempts to teach Arabic and to develop cultural activities, these projects have failed as much in the Club Palestino as in the Club El Prado. This has been due to the lack of a favorable response from the Palestinian-Salvadoran community. The Club has rather turned into a center for social gatherings where only a few cultural traditions, such as Arab music and dances, are preserved.[100]

Nowadays, Palestinian descendants in El Salvador are totally assimilated into the society of their host nation. They do not speak Arabic anymore and they consider themselves Salvadorans. Palestinian descendants can be found in all professional fields and in all activities and businesses. There are merchants, industrialists, physicians, lawyers, engineers, and so on. Nevertheless, this assimilation process was not an easy one in El Salvador, since there were many restrictions in the past, both for Palestinian immigrants and for their descendants as well. Despite that, many Palestinian-Salvadorans have been able to participate in politics and have occupied some important administrative positions, like the cases of José Arturo Zablah, who was Minister of Economy from 1989 to 1993.[101] Another example is Eduardo Zablah Touche, who was Minister of Economy of El Salvador from 1994 to 1998.[102] Two Palestinian descendants occupied the prestigious position of Mayor of Zacatecoluca: Jaime Fagrer, from 1924 to 1925; and Federico Alberto Hirezi, from 1953 to 1956.[103] José Zablah was director of CEPA (Comisión Ejecutiva Portuaria Autónoma) from 1994 to 1998.[104]

The president of ANTEL (Administración Nacional de Telecomunicaciones) was also of Palestinian background, Juan José Dabdoub 'Abdallah.[105]

The political problems in El Salvador and the guerrilla warfare that deeply affected this country during the 1980s had profound repercussions on Palestinian descendants.[106] Some were victims of terrorist actions and the guerilla warfare and were wounded. Others, less fortunate, died in those violent actions. This provoked a great exodus of Palestinian descendants from El Salvador to other countries in the area and to Miami. On the other hand, some Palestinian descendants in El Salvador identified themselves with the opposition groups and participated in the guerrilla warfare against the Salvadoran government. Among them is the case of Shafik Handal, a lawyer and expert in international politics, who was a member of the guerrillas in El Salvador for a number of years, mainly from the beginning of the civil war in 1980 to the peace accords in 1992.[107] This was also the case for some Palestinian descendants in Nicaragua who participated in the Sandinista revolution against the Somoza government and also supported the Palestinian revolution. In El Salvador many Palestinian descendants also agreed with the Palestinian revolution. Among them was the already mentioned Shafik Handal, who also was a member of the Salvadoran Communist Party and who occupied the important position of General Secretary of the party.[108] Shafik Handal became the hard line negotiator for the Farabundo Martí de Liberación Nacional (FMLN) with the Salvadoran government, led at the time by President Alfredo Cristiani.[109] Shafik Handal insisted that for the negotiations the Salvadoran armed forces should be reduced and transformed.[110] Handal was also one of the leaders responsible for changing the armed guerrillas into a political group, once they had disposed of their weapons. All of this was known during the negotiations between the guerrilla members and the representatives of the Cristiani administration, who met several times in San José, Costa Rica, in 1990.[111]

The signed peace agreement between the Salvadoran government and the guerrilla groups in 1987 and finally on 16 January 1992,[112] has opened a few new opportunities for the Palestinian-Salvadorans who were going back to the country. Shortly afterwards, Shafik Handal was a candidate for the Presidency of the Republic in 2004. However, another descendant of Palestinian immigrants in El Salvador, Antonio Saca, won the election as member of the official Partido Arena and became the first president of El Salvador of Palestinian descent. He was president from 2004 to 2009. His government was characterized by the right wing ideology and he was a clear defender of the Central America Free Trade Agreement (CAFTA) with the United States. However, intellectuals both in El Salvador and in Costa Rica strongly and bravely opposed the CAFTA, unfortunately to no avail.

During the Saca administration, there were two Salvadoran-Palestinians elected as congressmen from 2004 to 2009. They were Héctor Miguel Dada Hirezi (Partido Cambio Democrático) from San Salvador and Óscar Abraham Kattan Milla from Sonsonate. Likewise, Gerard Nasser Hasbun, a Salvadoran-Palestinian, was Deputy Mayor of the Municipality of San Salvador from 2006-2009.[113]

There were also some Palestinian-Salvadorans who moved to other Central American countries, such as Nijmeh (Estrella) Mu'ammar, who settled in Costa Rica along with her family. Her sons have recently returned to El Salvador to start various businesses.[114] In general, the most important contribution of the Palestinians in El Salvador has been at the economic level, for their clothing, footwear, and food businesses; their textile and salt industries; and their agricultural production in their lands. They have actively and successfully participated in politics and have also contributed at the financial level.

The Case of the Palestinians of Christian Origin in Nicaragua

It is hard to determine the number of Palestinians arriving in Nicaragua during the first decades of the twentieth century. Records are scarce, confusing, and erroneous about the Turkish nationality attributed to many of them. Our informants point out that it is possible to think that from the end of the nineteenth century until 1917 (during World War I), when the Ottoman Empire was in its final decline, 40 Palestinian families arrived in Nicaragua.[115] Nowadays, it is estimated that there are over 500 families of Palestinians and Palestinian descendants.[116]

The Palestinian immigrants in Nicaragua were mostly Christians. Some Muslims also arrived, although in smaller numbers, since only the Hasan and 'Abdallah families are known.[117] Palestinian immigrants in Nicaragua came from rural areas, mainly from villages near Ramallah and Jerusalem, as well as from Beit Jala and Bethlehem. Among the Palestinian Christians who arrived in Nicaragua was the family of the distinguished Palestinian-Nicaraguan poetess Suad Marcos Frech.[118] Some members of this family came from Bethlehem and others from Jerusalem. Among many other cities are the families of the Zogaib, Dajer, Farach, Karam, Aquel, Salty, Zarruk, and Hasbani.[119]

In spite of their rural origins and experience in agricultural work, Palestinian immigrants in Nicaragua devoted themselves to commerce, mainly clothing, footwear, and ornaments. Their trade activities brought them great profits. In Nicaragua, Palestinian immigrants settled in the main cities of Managua, Granada, and Masaya, where they founded their stores. As an example of a Palestinian family devoted to this activity, one can mention, among many other cases, that of the grandparents of Suad Marcos Frech, who were merchants in Managua.[120] Some of the most important stores founded by Palestinian immigrants or their descendants are: Tienda París Londres, Camisería Marcos, Almacén Dajer, La Media Luna, and Almacén Mónaco.[121] Only a small group of Palestinian immigrants, however, was able to buy land and to concentrate on agriculture, mainly in Sabana Grande, where from their earliest arrival they have produced cotton as well as various fruits such as manga china.[122] It is important to point out that later some of the Palestinian immigrants developed other economic interests such as manufacturing, mainly the textile industry. The Samara and Shijab[123] families are some examples of Palestinian families who have also devoted themselves to the textile industry. Furthermore, there are other industries, such as tomato sauce production.[124]

Since the end of the 1950s, Palestinians in Nicaragua started a club called Club Árabe (Arab Club), which was founded on 15 May 1958 with the purpose to attract other non-Palestinian Arabs. Even though about 80 per cent of the members of this club were Palestinians, there also were, according to our informants, some Syrians and some Lebanese.[125] This club allowed the Palestinian descendants in Nicaragua to preserve a certain cultural identity and to keep alive their ethnic origins.[126] This also seems to have been the tendency of some Palestinian-Nicaraguans who traveled to Palestine to obtain an education, as in the cases of Jacobo Marcos and Jorge Jacobo Marcos Bendeck.[127] There they acquired a clear political knowledge, a basic understanding of the Palestinian problems, and the need to defend the rights of the Palestinian people.[128] The same is also true for 'Issa Frech, who went to Palestine from 1972 to 1976 to learn Arabic.[129]

The second and third generations of Palestinians in Nicaragua are for the most part professionals. They have married Nicaraguan nationals and have Nicaraguan nationality. They no longer speak Arabic and are totally integrated into Nicaraguan society. Some members of the 'Abdallah family, for example, married women from Masaya and, in spite of being Muslims, their children were raised as Catholics, which is an indication of the rapid assimilation process in this host country. Among the professionals, there are engineers such as Carlos Zarruk, Salvador 'Abdallah, and Musa Hasan, the last of which even managed to occupy the prestigious office of Dean of the Faculty of Engineering[130] in the Universidad de Nicaragua in the 1970s.[131] There are also neurosurgeons and physicians, as in the cases of doctors Jacobo Marcos Frech, Moisés Hasan, Amín Hasan, Foad Hasan, William 'Abdallah, William Yudat Frech, and others; lawyers, as in the case of James Zablah; journalists like Anuar Hasan; and writers such as the poetess Suad Marcos Frech.[132]

It is important to underline the enormous political conscience of the Palestinians as a group in Nicaragua. Palestinians in this country, as in others, are clearly conscious of the sufferings of their Palestinian ancestors and relatives who have faced persecutions, discrimination, expulsions, and property and goods confiscation[133] by the Israeli military occupation of their territories.[134] For these reasons the Palestinian descendants in Nicaragua have also participated actively in Nicaraguan politics. Both the second and third generations of Palestinian immigrants in Nicaragua involved themselves directly in the struggle against the social and political injustices of the Anastasio Somoza Debayle regime (1967-1972 and 1974-1979). Some Palestinian descendants in Nicaragua, like Selim and Alberto Shibli, participated actively on the side of the Sandinistas before this group defeated the Somocistas and took power in June 1979. The same can also be pointed out with regard to the important role that the Palestinian-Nicaraguan poetess Suad Marcos Frech played in favor of the Sandinista revolution.[135]

Some Palestinian descendants came to occupy important administrative positions within the Sandinista Government Junta, as in the case of Musa Hasan. Others occupied ministerial positions: Jacobo Marcos Frech was Secretario General (General Secretary), position equivalent to Vice-Minister, in the Ministry of Health, from 1979 to 1982.[136] Carlos Zarruk was Defense Minister, James Zablah was Minister of Economy, and Suad Marcos Frech was Subdirectora of the National Penitentiary System, an office that belongs to the Ministry of the Interior, from 1979 to 1980.[137] Another Palestinian descendant who occupied an important administrative and political position was Sucre Frech, who was Sports Minister. He died in 1991.[138] Yasser 'Arafat, then president of the PLO, even sent a letter of condolence from Tunisia to Sucre''s family, dated 29 January 1991.[139]

On the other hand, the confiscations and the nationalization process of the Sandinista government forced the exodus of some Palestinian-Nicaraguans, as in the case of the Samara family, who affirmed to have lost properties and businesses that were confiscated by that regime. The Samara family then moved to Costa Rica where they have a business in clothing, footwear, and other items.

The Sandinistas opened for the first time a PLO diplomatic representation in Managua (1981), the first diplomatic seat of the Palestinian representation in Central America, which was until recently the only one. This diplomatic seat reflects the changes, views, and perceptions of Nicaragua in the international sphere towards the defense of the rights of the Palestinian people. As a contrast, other countries in the area, namely Costa Rica[140] and El Salvador, moved their Embassies from Tel Aviv to Jerusalem in the early 1980s, acknowledging this city as the capital of Israel. These two Embassies in Jerusalem passively supported the legality of a military occupation in detriment of the Palestinian rights and in clear opposition to the United Nations accords that call for the internationalization of Jerusalem.[141] However, in 2006, Costa Rica, later followed by El Salvador, moved their Embassies back to Tel Aviv, complying with the numerous United Nations resolutions, and with a strong determination to advocate the rights of the Palestinian people. This political change also meant a rejection of the Israeli military occupation of the Palestinian territories, as well as a protest against the Israeli military abuses and constant violation of human rights in Palestine. The PLO's representation in Managua continues today with five assigned functionaries, which constitutes a reduced number. At the times of the Sandinistas, this Palestinian diplomatic office had up to thirty members. Four leading functionaries of the Palestinian diplomatic office in Managua have fulfilled important tasks in Nicaragua: Marwan Tarbub (from 1981 to 1989), 'Abd al-'Aziz al-Aftal (1989-1990), Musa Amer Odeh (1990-1992), George 'Issa Salamah (1992), and Walid al-Mu'aqat (2008 to the present).[142]

The Case of the Palestinians of Christian Origin in Costa Rica

Arab immigrants in Costa Rica during the first period of immigration, from the late nineteenth century until World War I, and during the second period between the World Wars, included mainly Lebanese and Syrians. Very few Palestinians of Christian origin came to Costa Rica during these two periods of immigration. Only Rafael Zakariyya (Zacarías) Bakit (Bakhit), 'Isa Ibrahim (Salvador Abraham) Hasbun Hasbun and his cousin 'Isa (Salvador) Jorge Hasbun are known to have arrived. Rafael Zacarías Bakit (Bakhit), who came from 'Ayn Karim, near Jerusalem, arrived in 1909 with his brother.[143] Both started a business in Puerto Limón, but when his brother returned to Palestine, Zacarías moved to San José where he took up the representation of foreign pharmaceutical houses, a job he successfully performed because, among many other reasons, he was fluent in six languages and had a fair communication level in four others. He was also the owner of the elegant Royal Bar, which for many years attracted the most distinguished politicians, academics, and journalists of the country to important intellectual conversations. Bakit was Catholic and was registered as such in the records in Costa Rica, though he was given Syrian nationality. Zacarías Bakit died in Managua from an earthquake in 1931.[144] 'Isa Ibrahim (Salvador Abraham) Hasbun Hasbun arrived in Costa Rica from El Salvador early in 1941.[145] In El Salvador, where he arrived in 1924, he devoted himself to commerce with a small store in San Miguel.[146] In El Salvador he met another Palestinian, Warde (Rosa) Hasbun Dabdoub, whom he married in 1932.[147] Moreover, after meeting Ricardo Saprissa, a businessman owner of a textile factory in Costa Rica, Salvador Hasbun moved to this other country in Central America, where he settled in Lepanto in the province of Puntarenas. He devoted himself to cotton production in order to provide raw material for the Saprissa textile factory,[148] but due to the unhealthy conditions of the region of Lepanto he contracted malaria. And so Salvador Hasbun left the region and cotton production and started his own cattle-raising business, which was unsuccessful.[149] He then moved to the province of Cartago, where he had a restaurant, and he later left Cartago with his family and settled in the province of Limón on the Caribbean coast. There he founded a sawmill, which he kept for many years.[150] It turned out to be a prosperous business.[151] His cousin, 'Isa (Salvador) Jorge Hasbun, arrived in Costa Rica from El Salvador, also in 1941.[152] By that time he had already married Anisse 'Isa Hasbun Nassar.[153] Salvador Jorge Hasbun performed different activities in Costa Rica. At first he started a textile factory in the province of Cartago, which was not a successful business,[154] so he had to close it down and moved to the province of Puntarenas, where he devoted himself to agriculture. Later, as did his cousin 'Isa Ibrahim, he moved to the province of Guanacaste for cattle-raising. This was not a sound business either, and he decided to go back to Cartago to assist his cousin in the restaurant La Florida.[155] For the remainder of his life Salvador Jorge Hasbun devoted himself to the itinerant commerce of grains and other foods in the southern regions of the country. He carried produce from Cartago to San Isidro de El General and to other cities in that area.[156]

There were, then, very few Costa Ricans of Palestinian origin who settled in this country during the first two periods of the Arab immigration to Latin America, with the exceptions of the descendants of Zacarías Bakit and those of Salvador Abraham Hasbun Hasbun.[157] Two daughters of Salvador Hasbun, Leyla Hasbun and Mayra Hasbun, are English professors. Leyla Hasbun has taught at the University of Costa Rica since 1980, while Mayra Hasbun has taught at the Universidad Hisponoamericana since 1989 and at the Universidad Latina since 1992.[158] The reasons for the scarcity of Palestinian immigrants in Costa Rica at a time when many of their countrymen settled in other Central American nations are unknown. Any explanation would be pure speculation. It is possible that Palestinians found better economic opportunities in the other countries of the area, which acted as an incentive for their settlement in those nations that offered the best possibilities. In 1904, Ascensión Esquivel, then President of the Republic, issued an executive decree (number 1 of 10 June 1904) prohibiting the entry to Costa Rica of Arabs, Turks, Syrians, Armenians, and Gypsies of any nationality, which was an impediment for many more Palestinians to arrive to Costa Rica.[159]

In Costa Rica there are 32 households of Palestinian origin. There are 31 families and one single man from Palestine. The majority of them arrived after the Israeli occupation of the territories of Gaza and the West Bank in 1967, especially in the early 1970s, even though there were some sporadic cases before that year. Among these cases was Alberto Bakit from 'Ayn Karim and cousin of Zacarías, who arrived in 1963. Alberto Bakit stayed in Costa Rica for a short period and very soon moved to Chile.[160] The majority of the most recent Palestinian immigrants in Costa Rica, mainly after the major wars of the Arab-Israeli conflict, are Muslims. Therefore, their political participation and economic success are beyond the scope of this essay. However, on the whole, most of the Palestinian immigrants and their descendants in Costa Rica are Christians of various denominations. This is shown in the following table:

Table No. 2

Religions of the Palestinians and Palestinian descendants in Costa Rica

Religions	Number	Percentage
Catholics	55	52.38
Muslims	24	22.86
Orthodox	20	19.05
Other Christian denominations	1	0.95
Not Declared	5	4.76
Total	105	100 %

Source: Information gathered by the author through interviews (1993-1996), (2009-2010)

From an economic point of view, the Palestinians have contributed to the progress of certain areas of the country, even though on a modest scale. An example is the case of the small farm for coffee and citrus production in Turrialba owned by Dr. 'Abd al-Fattah Sa'sa', a Muslim, or the cattle farm owned by Nijmeh (Estrella) Mu'ammar in the area near San Carlos. The extension of this farm is 100 hectares (1 hectare is 2.47 acres) and today has over 100 heads of cattle.[161] Others in their businesses have also generated jobs, as in the case of the jewellers Mauricio Sayegh, his brother Elías, and his nephew Raja Bakkar.[162] Furthermore, one can mention the case of Hajj Hanna Frech who is the owner of a store for clothing, footwear, and house utensils in San José, which is administrated by his son 'Issa Frech.[163] Hanna Frech also owns another similar store in the border area between Costa Rica and Panama.[164]

Oscar Bakit had, until his death in 1998, a very active business life with his Bakit de Centro America, an advertising company divided in three parts:
1. An accounting enterprise;
2. Telepress, for television news, similar to a news agency;
3. IDEAS (International Development of Enterprises of Advertising and Sales), the advertising enterprise, which actually designs and publishes ads in different newspapers and other media for different companies.[165]

All these three professional businesses have generated 28 permanent new jobs and 10 temporary jobs. Michael Canavati (Qanawati) is a Palestinian industrialist in Costa Rica. He has the Lovable factory for women's underwear. This factory has generated 210 new jobs in Costa Rica.[166] The Lovable factory is also located in Honduras where it is one of the major industries for women's underwear. Its products are sold in all the countries of Central America.[167] Michael Canavati (Qanawati) is also the owner of Monty's, an entertainment center and tourist resort in San Joaquín de Flores, in the province of Heredia. This center has created 55 new jobs.[168] Yusuf Samara, a Muslim, added to the industrial activities with his Creaciones Yiris factory, especially for women's underwear. This factory has also generated employment in Costa Rica.[169] According to the information, Creaciones Yiris has created 45 new jobs in the country.[170]

Some Palestinians, such as Michael Canavati and Norma Handal from Honduras and the various Hasbun families from El Salvador, have arrived in Costa Rica from other countries of Central America. Some others were Muslims, such as 'Abd al-Karim Tahir, who arrived from Panama,[171] Kamal Rishmawi, who arrived from Honduras, and Yusuf and Halima Samara, from Nicaragua. Several factors have contributed to this more local immigration. Among them are marriage, as in the case of Nijmeh (Estrella) Mu'ammar who married to a Costa Rican, or the political difficulties and internal conflict in some of the other countries of Central America that caused some Palestinians to move to Costa Rica in search of better conditions and peace.[172] Related to the issue of marriage, it is necessary to explain that from the first two Palestinian immigrants in Costa Rica, Zakariyya Bakit and 'Isa Ibrahim Hasbun, only one of them, the latter, married a Palestinian woman. This is the first example of endogamy among Palestinians in Costa Rica. However, since they met and married in El Salvador before moving to Costa Rica, this process can also be understood as a case of a Palestinian family moving to Costa Rica. Bakit married a Costa Rican woman, therefore initiating the blood mixture. Both descendant families, Bakit and Hasbun, in the second and third generations, married Costa Ricans. This was mainly due to the fact that there were very few Palestinian descendants in Costa Rica, and they did not keep the tradition to look for distant (or close) cousins for possible marriages arranged by their respective families, as it has been preserved, although with some limitations, among Palestinian descendants in Honduras and Nicaragua, for example.[173]

The majority of the Palestinian immigrants of Christian origin who arrived in Costa Rica during the seventies and afterwards constitute mixed marriages, either with Costa Ricans or other Central Americans. Among them are the cases of Elías Raja, married to a Costa Rican; Michael Qanawati, married to a Honduran woman; and José Jorge Marcos Frech, married (later divorced) a Nicaraguan woman. However, some Palestinian immigrants are married to other Palestinians, like the case of Hajj Hanna Frech who is married to a Palestinian woman. Raja Sayegh is also married to a Palestinian woman. These are the examples of endogamy. On the other hand, there are other examples of Arab endogamy, although not absolutely Palestinian, like the cases of Dr. Norma Handal, a Palestinian immigrant from Bethlehem to Honduras, and later to Costa Rica, who is married to a Costa Rican of Lebanese origin. Other examples of Arab endogamy are the cases of Mauricio Sayegh, who is married to a Lebanese woman, and 'Issa Frech, a second generation of Palestinian origin, who arrived in Costa Rica from Nicaragua, and is married to a Jordanian woman.

In the political and diplomatic spheres, some Palestinian descendants have distinguished themselves in the Costa Rican foreign service. Dr. Jorge Hasbun has occupied diplomatic positions abroad. He was first Counsellor of the Embassy of Costa Rica in Argentina from 1990 to 1992 and was then appointed Ambassador of Costa Rica to Romania from 1993 to 1994.[174]

The second and third generations of Palestinian immigrants are completely assimilated with the Costa Rican culture and values, as this process has occurred with other Arab immigrants in Costa Rica, in the other countries of Central America, and in many other nations in the world. The loss of the Arabic language as the main vehicle for communication and the preservation of cultural ties from one generation to the other could have contributed as one of the major reasons for the whole process. Undoubtedly, the second and third generations of Palestinian immigrants are mainly the result of the blending, through wedding links, of Palestinians with Costa Ricans. Many of the Palestinian descendants have studied in Costa Rica and have become professionals in different fields. For example, Doreen Bakit studied Painting in the Fine Arts Department of the University of Costa Rica. Her brother, Christian Bakit, graduated in Advertising and today works in his profession.[175] Norma Handal is also a professional and works as a psychiatrist. The cases of the Hasbun sisters, already mentioned, as teachers of English is also relevant, as well as the cases of Gerardo Solorzano Bakit, who studied Business Administration in the Universidad Latina, and Alberto Solorzano Bakit, who studied Veterinary Science at the Universidad Nacional in Heredia, Costa Rica.[176]

These are just a few examples of the professional developments of Palestinian immigrants and their descendants in Costa Rica.[177] Through education as well as through the Christian religion, since the majority of the Costa Rican population practice Catholicism, descendants of Palestinian immigrants have accomplished a complete integration into Costa Rican society. The same tendency of assimilation into the national culture of the host country and total loss of the Arabic language can be seen, with few exceptions, from the second and third generations of Palestinian immigrants in Costa Rica and also in other countries in Central America.[178]

The Case of the Palestinians of Christian Origin in Guatemala

Palestinians arriving in Guatemala since the late nineteenth century and especially in the early twentieth century coincided with the arrival of many of their countrymen in other nations in Central America. They entered in small numbers and did not maintain a group unity or a strong cultural identity,[179] as has been possible to determine for the Palestinian immigrants in Honduras or Nicaragua, or for those of more recent arrival in Costa Rica. These few Palestinians in Guatemala have accomplished economic success, mainly in commerce and the textile industry. In the case of commerce, the Abularach family, the first one of Palestinian origin and Christian faith to arrive to Guatemala, was successful in business from the very beginning. This family concentrated especially in the import-export business.[180] As early as 1914, Garza Abularach requested a tax exemption to import 50 looms, 25 other machines, and a steam-operated kettlemaker for a clothing factory, proof of his family's fast growing economic prosperity.[181]

The Safie family has also been successful in different businesses in Guatemala, as well as in the textile industry. The Safie still owns one of the major clothing factories in Central America, called La Estrella. This family has been successful as merchants as well. The Zibara family was also devoted to commerce since their early arrival to Guatemala. They had their major shops in the Portal del Señor, an important commercial area in Guatemala City, where today the Palacio Nacional is located. The descendants of the first Zibara members who settled in Guatemala are also devoted to the textile industry. The Zibara, as well as the Abularach and the Dacaret families, also owned warehouses and participated in local and administrative politics. Education was a means to excel for these families. Some of them have become members of the professional class since the early 1940s. Undoubtedly, education has contributed to their rapid integration and assimilation into the Guatemalan society. They frequently married Guatemalan women, mainly due to the limited presence of Palestinians in the country.[182]

Palestinian descendants in Guatemala have distinguished themselves in various cultural and artistic fields, like the case of the renowned painter Rodolfo Abularach. In politics, one has to mention the case of Emilio Saca Dabdoub, a member of the right wing Partido de Avanzada Nacional (PAN), who was elected as a congressman for the period 1996-2000, during the presidency of Alvaro Arzú Irigoyen. The president of Guatemala even appointed him as his Private Secretary of the Presidency. Nowadays Palestinian descendants in Guatemala do not speak Arabic; they consider themselves Guatemalans and are totally assimilated into the culture of this host country. This does not mean that they did not support or talk in favor of the PLO in the past, or more recently in favor of the Palestinian National Authority and the possible creation of a Palestinian State. However, they have been very careful and they never published an article or went into the television news to express an idea as a group, but rather as individuals. As a community, and because they live in Guatemala, they assert that their presence, as well as the presence of Jews in the country, should not parallel the Arab-Israeli conflict. Palestinians reject having any kind of problems with other Guatemalans, including Jews. This attitude has avoided breaking out hostilities between the two communities.

Conclusion

After the case studies analyzed in this essay, it is possible to conclude that there are specificities and particularities for each group of Palestinian immigrants in the five Central American republics. There are also special characteristics for each particular period of immigration. In this diverse environment, one can observe general patterns as explained in this essay. The first Palestinian immigrants in Central America arrived in the late nineteenth and early twentieth centuries. The largest number of Palestinian immigrants went to Honduras. These Palestinian immigrants were mainly of rural origin and were Christians. They went to Central America in search of better economic conditions and religious and political freedom. Syrians arrived under similar conditions as the Palestinians. Most of the Palestinians, but also some other Arab immigrants in Central America, mainly the Lebanese, devoted themselves to commerce, first itinerant and later in urban stores. Some Palestinian immigrants of Christian origin in Central America, as was demonstrated by the examples of Guatemala, El Salvador, and Honduras, became involved in industrial activities, mainly textiles. In some countries of Central America, like Costa Rica and Nicaragua, Palestinian industrial activities have been on a modest scale, since commerce has always been their main activity. The economic success of the Palestinian immigrants allowed them not only to quickly ascend the social ladder in these host Central American nations, but also to send money to Palestine to help their families or to pay for the entire trip expenses to bring over relatives and friends. These financial contributions also improved the economic condition of the towns and villages they left behind in Palestine. This was reported by various Ottoman administrative authorities and also by some European consular representatives.[183]

Palestinian descendants of Christian origin in Central America from the first period of immigration are found completely integrated in the countries that admitted their ancestors. Some of them, mainly the Christians, have adopted Spanish common names, and have participated in politics as congressmen, ministers, mayors, and diplomats. Carlos Flores-Facusse and Antonio Saca were even elected as presidents of Honduras and El Salvador, respectively. These immigrants do not speak Arabic and have accelerated, by means of education and their economic activities, the integration process into the society and culture of the various host countries. Presently, in Honduras, El Salvador, Nicaragua, and Guatemala, and less visibly in Costa Rica, there are Palestinian descendants in a wide variety of professional, artistic, cultural, scientific, sports, industrial, financial, and commercial activities. More recent Palestinian immigrants have arrived in search of better living conditions due to political problems and economic crisis in the Middle East. The general pattern that can be observed in this new group of Palestinian immigrants after the foundation of the State of Israel (1948) and the Israeli military occupation of Gaza and the West Bank (1967) is their greater intellectual preparation, their urban origins, and their clear desire to defend the rights of the Palestinian people. Most of these new and more recent immigrants are Muslims, although there are some Christians too. Some others have emigrated to these Central American republics due to their marriages to citizens of these countries. This has created matrimonial liaisons mixed in religion, culture, and ethnic group.[184]

In Central America, the second, the third, and in certain cases even the fourth generation of Palestinian descendants have lost the Arabic language. Still, they have a clear desire to defend the Palestinian people and to rescue the Arab cultural values and traditions. For that matter, they have founded cultural organizations and have published newspapers, bulletins, and magazines with the intention to preserve and spread Arab cultural values and traditions in these countries. Likewise, they attempt to accomplish a greater understanding and solidarity between the national communities and the Arab immigrants and their descendants.

Palestinian Diaspora in Central America
- A Story of Hardship and Success[185]-

Manzar Foroohar

Since the beginning of the twentieth century, a large number of Palestinians and their descendants, who live in different Central American countries as part of the Palestinian international diaspora, have played a major role in the social, cultural, and economic development of their Central American host countries. Despite that, however, Palestinians are almost invisible in Central American historiography. Only a few Latin Americanists have attempted to study the history of Palestinian immigration to Central America and its impact on the socioeconomic and cultural formation of the region.[186]

This chapter is an attempt to document the previously neglected history of the Palestinian diaspora in Central America. It focuses on the history of the formation of Palestinian communities in the region and the social, economic, and political contributions they have made to their adopted countries. The paper is based on existing documentation as well as interviews that were made with the immigrants and their descendants in Central America and/or with persons "back home" familiar with the emigration. While Palestinian communities throughout Central America will be discussed, particular attention will be paid to Honduras and El Salvador; the countries with the largest concentration of Palestinians in the region.

The Early Immigrants

Palestinian immigration to Central America began at the end of the nineteenth century. Because Palestine, like most of the Arab Middle East, was under Ottoman rule until 1918, it is difficult to document the numbers of immigrants accurately since they carried Ottoman (Turkish) passports and therefore were categorized in the Central American registries as Turks (turcos). Although some documentation of the Palestinian component of Arab immigration exists for Honduras, where Palestinians are shown to constitute the overwhelming majority,[187] no such information is available for the other states of the region.

The majority of the early Palestinian immigrants were young men who belonged to Christian communities in Palestine, especially around the Bethlehem-Jerusalem area. Highlighting the

Christian faith of the majority of early immigrants, some scholars point to religious persecution of Christian minorities as an important factor in the early emigration out of Palestine.[188] However, there is no historical proof of this assertion, and most historians of the Middle East point to the general economic decline of the Ottoman Empire and the ongoing wars as the main reasons for emigration of both Christian and Muslim citizens of the Empire. They argue that, because of religious identification, the majority of Muslim Ottoman emigrants preferred to move to Egypt whereas the Christians moved to Christian countries in the West, where they could easily blend into Christian communities and churches.[189]

There is a general agreement among the historians about the impact of the economic decline of the Ottoman Empire during the late nineteenth and early twentieth centuries on emigration of Palestinians and other citizens of the Empire. Under the Ottoman rule, agriculture was neglected for centuries. The peasants' lack of knowledge of agricultural technology and pest control combined with inadequate rainfall resulted in a gradual decline of the agriculture. Added to these problems were foreign competition, lack of security in the countryside, constant threat of Bedouin raids, and peasants' defenselessness against the greed of Ottoman tax collectors. The life of the Ottoman peasant was getting progressively more difficult in the second half of the nineteenth century.

The traditional industries, especially in textile sector, were also declining in the nineteenth century in the face of foreign competition. Low tariffs on foreign imports, imposed on the Ottoman Empire due to "capitulation" agreements with European powers, flooded the market with cheap foreign textile, and caused a process of decline for domestic silk and cotton textile industries. Another factor in the decline of traditional industries was the opening of the Suez Canal in 1869, which not only hurt the traditional trading routs in the Ottoman Empire, but also facilitated transportation of Japanese and Chinese silk to Europe and effectively pushed the Ottoman textile out of the international markets.

Constant wars, especially WWI, also hurt the Ottoman economy. The new conscription law, enacted in 1908, intensified the wave of emigration among young male citizens of the Empire.[190] In interviews with descendants of early immigrants, two factors were repeatedly pointed out as the main reasons for early emigration: miserable economic conditions during the war, and the military draft obligations.[191]

General conditions in the home country explain the main characteristics and the motifs of Arab emigrants who arrived in Central America in the late nineteenth and early twentieth centuries. The early emigrants were generally young males, 15 to 30 years old, looking for an opportunity to prosper in a foreign land. A majority wanted to return home after saving money. Writing about early Syrian [including Palestinians and Lebanese] immigrants to the United States, Philip Hitti, argues that "the ideal of the first immigrants to the United States was to amass all the wealth possible in the shortest time and then return to Syria to enjoy it in peace and quietude."[192]

Although it is difficult to calculate the number of emigrants who returned home following a brief period of emigration, some scholars believe that "between one-third to one-half of the early emigrants returned home and invested their savings in land and new homes."[193]

The returning emigrants' wealth and prosperity was a new factor in encouraging the local population, especially young men, to follow suit and try their luck in foreign ventures. Returning emigrants also acted as information sources about foreign countries and economic opportunities in the Americas.

Local steamship-company agents facilitated the emigration, arranging transport for emigrants from villages and towns to major ports, and from there to Europe and then the Americas.[194] The journey to Central America would take one to three months in small, poorly ventilated cabins under deplorable conditions.[195] According to accounts by early immigrants and their descendants, many had originally wanted to go to the United States and had purchased their passages accordingly. But as the first stop of ships from Europe to the Americas was a port either in the Caribbean or in Central America, some were simply deposited there despite the promises by the travel agents, and told they had reached their final destination.[196] Interviews with the descendants of Palestinian immigrants to Central America, over and over, pointed to arrival sites such as Port of Corinto in Nicaragua and Puerto Limon in Costa Rica as places the immigrants were left by the boats that were supposed to take them to the United States.[197]

The attraction of the United States for the early Palestinian emigrants was, at least partially, due to the success of Palestinian merchants participating in international expositions in the United States such as the Philadelphia Exposition of 1876, the Chicago fair of 1893, and the St. Luis exhibition of 1906. Philip Hitti, one of the first historians writing about Arab immigration to the Americas, describes the Columbian Exposition of 1893 (in Chicago) as "constituting the first general bugle call to the land of opportunity." According to Hitti, "the exposition is known to have attracted especially traders from Jerusalem and Ramallah who brought with them olive wood articles and other curios."[198] Najib Saliba affirms that "there are abundant references to the importance of those fairs in attracting and spreading immigrants all over the country. Among the Syrian [including Palestinian] goods displayed were icons, strings of beads, and crosses, items for which Palestine was noted."[199]

Adnan Musallam reports the accounts told by the descendants of the early immigrants as follows: "According to oral traditions, Bethlehemites Geries Ibrahim Suleiman Mansoor Handal, Geries Anton Abul-'Arraj, Hanna Khalil Moros, and Mishel and Gabriel Dabdoub and others attended these international exhibitions. The Handal brothers eventually settled down in New York while the Dabdoub brothers, who received a medal during the Chicago Exhibition, returned to their native town."[200] These merchants not only were successful in exhibiting and selling their merchandise, but they also established connections with their counterparts from other American countries and gathered information on the possibility of selling their crafts in those countries. It is possible that strong religious beliefs in Central America and demand for religious objects made in the Holy Land encouraged Palestinian merchants to explore the possibility of trade with, and immigration to, Central American countries.

Although there is no documentation of the first Palestinian who arrived in Central America, several descendants of Palestinian immigrants in San Pedro Sula, Honduras, recount the story of a Palestinian who entered Cutuco Port in El Salvador and left from Acajutla Port in the 1890s.[201] The Honduran scholar, Dario Euraque, identifies Salomon Handal as the first documented case of a Palestinian immigrant residing in San Pedro Sula in 1899.[202] The first documented Palestinian female immigrant, Rosa Handal, a native of Bethlehem who became involved in trade, arrived in San Pedro Sula in December 1898 at the age of 17.[203]

Most Palestinians who came to Central America in the late nineteenth and early twentieth centuries did not arrive directly from the Middle East. Some were born in Caribbean countries such as Haiti, the Dominican Republic, and Cuba, or in South American countries such as Chile and Colombia.

The majority of early immigrants were Christians from the Bethlehem-Jerusalem area. Although there were cases of Muslim immigrants from the beginning of the immigration process, the Muslim communities did not take root in the area, and there was no major Muslim Palestinian community in the region until the second half of the twentieth century. In addition to the total absence of mosques as a deterrent to settlement, cultural and social traditions also played a role. With few Muslim women making the journey, many Muslim men who decided to stay married local women, their children being baptized as Catholics.[204]

The existing historiography on Palestinian immigration generally assumes that the early emigrants were poor peasants.[205] Tracing the family roots of early immigrants back in Palestine, however, reveals the fallacy of this generalization. Many early immigrants to Central America, especially those who settled in Honduras and El Salvador, came from the urban areas of Bethlehem and lived very close to the center of the old city of Bethlehem. A visit to Bethlehem demonstrates a well-established urban background for families such as Handal, Hazbun, and Giacaman (Yakaman), whose old residential family compounds are still used by family members in the old city. The structure and location of these residences contradict the claim that these emigrants were poor peasants. Although most of these families also owned farming lands, their main economic activities were based on commerce.[206] Some of these families had long-established workshops and stores in the Holy Land, especially in Bethlehem and Jerusalem, in which they were producing and selling religious and other small souvenirs made of olive wood and mother-of-pearl. Their main customers were the thousands of international tourists visiting the Holy Land every year. It was thus natural that when Palestinians arrived in the Americas, they would work in areas related to their background in trade. Many started out as itinerant salesmen, often selling small religious items from the Holy Land that were very popular among Central American Catholics, before branching out and developing new lines of trade. Most were either single men or had wives and children still in Palestine. Even those who established businesses and decided to remain in Central America maintained close ties with their families back home, returning to Palestine either to marry Palestinian women to join them or to fetch their families. Since the majority of early immigrants perceived their situation as temporary and wanted to return to their homeland, they did not invest in agriculture, which usually signifies plans for permanent residency.

Another notion widely accepted by Central and North American scholars is the assumption that the majority of Palestinian immigrants were uneducated. Again an examination of the history of Palestine, especially in the Bethlehem-Jerusalem area, demonstrates the fallacy of this generalization. Although during the Ottoman Empire the majority of Muslim Palestinians were poor peasants living in rural areas with limited access to education,[207] a large number of Christian Palestinians lived in urban areas and had much higher access to education. In contrast to lack of educational institutions in rural areas, Palestinian cities, especially Jerusalem and Bethlehem, were dotted with missionary schools that educated the children of Christian Palestinian families. During the Ottoman rule, especially in the nineteenth century, European powers considered the missionary schools as a useful vehicle to increase their power and promote their interests in the region. These schools were established and controlled by such varied bodies as "the Church Missionary Society, the Jerusalem and East Mission, the Scots Mission, the Swedish Mission, and numerous Roman Catholic missions. In addition, other schools were maintained by local ecclesiastical and lay authorities, notably the Roman Catholic and Orthodox."[208] The first missionary educational institution in Palestine was established in 1645 in Jerusalem by the Order of the Friars Minor.[209] Missionary schools in Palestine were not limited to elementary schools but provided a comprehensive educational program.

Commercial Success

Following an early period of hardship, Palestinian immigrants to Central America established prosperous businesses and, in a relatively short time span, joined the dominant class in the commercial structure of their host countries. In the late 1910s in San Pedro Sula, for example, Arab merchants, 95% of them Palestinians, "controlled major sectors of the city's elite structure, especially large commerce."[210]

There were different reasons for the commercial success of Palestinian immigrants in Central America. This success was, at least partially, the result of existing conditions in the region when the immigrants arrived. Central American economic culture in the nineteenth and early twentieth centuries was a continuation of the system established by Spanish colonialism. The Iberian colonialism in Latin America brought to the new world a socioeconomic system based on large landownership and landed aristocracy. The upper class of colonial Latin America had a deep disdain for commercial and banking activities. Devaluation of business activities by the upper class created a void in the economic system that was easily filled by immigrants, including Palestinians. They arrived at a time when economic growth, in the framework of liberal capitalism, needed a merchant class to meet the demands of a growing market economy. Palestinian immigrants, as outsiders, were not constrained by the cultural norms of the host societies and easily established themselves in businesses that, although highly profitable, were not valued in the existing culture as jobs suitable for the rich and privileged.[211]

To study the remarkable economic success of Palestinian immigrants in Central America, I will focus on Honduras,[212] where a large part of commercial and industrial network of the country is dominated by descendants of Palestinian immigrants.

During the colonial period, Honduras had a poor subsistence-based economy. Following the independence and until the 1870s, the small scale export economy was based on minerals, especially gold and silver, and hardwood and cattle. Foreign investment in the country was very small and remained limited well into the first decade of the twentieth century. Although several North American mining companies, including New York and Rosario Mining Company, invested in Honduras, their activities did not benefit the country for several reasons. First, mining was limited to the areas around Tegucigalpa and did not expand to the rest of the country. Second, the numbers of workers in these mines were rarely more than 1500, and third, government decrees and concessions granted these companies tax exemptions well into the 1940s. Although the export of silver counted for 10 to 25 percent of Honduran exports, the country could not enjoy any major economic benefits from mining due to the tax exemption status of the companies.

For the most part, the Honduran economy, even in the late nineteenth century, was still traditional and pre-capitalist. In contrast to Guatemala, El Salvador, and Costa Rica, where expansion of coffee production transformed the economic structure in the second half of the nineteenth century, Honduras remained mostly a subsistence economy until the arrival of the North American banana companies in the beginning of the twentieth century. Economic stagnation and political fragmentation in the nineteenth century impeded the formation of a local bourgeoisie that would be able to respond to the demands of the external market or to form a productive system with significant national participation, as was the case for example in Costa Rica, where the growth of banana production always took second place after the nationally controlled coffee production sector.[213]

The Honduran economic elite, which had not been able to transform itself from a traditional oligarchy to a capitalist class, could not lead nor had any major impact on the economic development of the country. Thus when the growth of banana production on the north coast changed the area to a rapidly growing economy, it was the immigrants, especially Arab Palestinians, who functioned as the merchant class and inserted themselves in the economic system filling the void.

The early Palestinian immigrants to Honduras settled in cities on the north coast such as La Lima, El Progreso and Puerto Cortés, where the banana industries were flourishing and providing opportunities for commerce. These immigrants lived modestly and invested their money in their business. Most of the single men rented a room with almost no furniture. When married, most of the early Palestinian immigrants lived in residences in the back or above their shops.[214] The Palestinian immigrants also helped their relatives and friends to immigrate to Honduras. There was a widely accepted practice of helping new immigrants by offering them jobs, housing, and low interest loans to start their own businesses. This practice created a community of successful merchants and industrialists with many members, instead of a few with large concentration of capital. In his study of the city of San Pedro Sula and the north coast of Honduras in the 1930s, Dario Euraque observes, "Unlike the Hondurans, and in fact unlike all other foreigners involved in San Pedro Sula's elite commerce, by the 1930s the total Arab investments were distributed widely among many merchants and regions, not only in Cortés but elsewhere on the North Coast... None of the European or US citizens matched the range and distribution network established by the Arabs."[215] Although the passage of time and integration into the host societies have weakened the close family ties in forming and maintaining business associations, Central American Palestinians have preserved, at least partially, the tradition of family and ethnic cooperation in their economic activities.

The liberal immigration policies of most Central American countries, especially Honduras, helped the increase in chain immigration of Palestinians and their relatives. As in other Central American countries, the liberal governments of Honduras promoted foreign immigration as a means to social, cultural, and economic progress. Although the intention of the nineteenth century liberals was to promote European and North American immigration, the 1866 and 1906 immigration laws in Honduras did not specify any race or nationality as "preferred" immigrants, and, as such, opened the country to immigrants from different backgrounds and nationalities, including Arabs.

Although the Honduran central government and local authorities, eager to attract foreign immigration to develop the economy, offered land grants to immigrants, most Palestinians chose commercial activities over agriculture for reasons discussed elsewhere in this chapter. They functioned as itinerant peddlers and salesmen roaming the rural areas and urban neighborhoods, selling household necessities to Honduran housewives and agricultural tools to farmers.

Most early Palestinian immigrants were educated in missionary schools in Palestine, especially in Bethlehem. Some who were involved in trade and tourism in the Holy Land had the advantage of familiarity with different languages. Jacobo Katan, a Palestinian merchant who arrived in San Pedro Sula in 1914, for example, spoke Arabic, English, French, Italian, and Spanish and served his diverse clients in different languages.[216] Also a majority of female Palestinian immigrants were educated before arriving in Honduras.[217]

By the second decade of the twentieth century, Palestinian merchants were already in control of the commercial network of the city of San Pedro Sula. A review of taxes paid by shops in San Pedro Sula in 1918 reveals that about 47.5 percent of sales tax was paid by the city's Arab shop owners. Honduran shop owners accounted for only 2.5 percent of taxes.[218]

Control of the San Pedro Sula commercial sector by Palestinians was firmly established by the 1930s. The list of owners of the city's most important commercial establishments included Larach, Canahuati, Sahuri, Saybe, Yacaman, Handal, Kawas, and other Palestinian names.[219] The Palestinian control over the commercial system was especially salient in the import/export sector. According to the Mercantile Registry of Cortés for 1919-1936 (Registro Mercantil de Cortés), Arabs controlled 67 percent of the investment value registered in the import and export sector of San Pedro Sula. Hondurans controlled only five percent.[220] The only part of the commercial network controlled by the Hondurans was the network of neighborhood grocery stores in San Pedro Sula and other parts of the North Coast, which were heavily dependent on the supplies from larger general stores controlled by Palestinians.

In the 1920s, Palestinian merchants expanded their economic activities into small-scale industries and invested in the newly established industrial sector on the north coast. Most industrial establishments of San Pedro Sula in the 1920s and 1930s were joint ventures, but, when it came to individual investments in industry, the Arabs surpassed other immigrants and Honduran industrialists. The focus of most early Palestinian industrial activities was apparel production. In 1929, for example, the city's two most important textile factories belonged to Palestinians. One of them, Jacobo Kattan, who had lived in the city since 1914, established La Sampedrana, a business producing men's clothing. The other major factory, La Perfección, established in 1921, belonged to the Andonie Family.[221]

Palestinian control over the commercial network of the north coast was later expanded to the rest of the country. Before WWII, German immigrants controlled a major part of the commercial network in central and southern parts of the country. During WWII, with the return of Germans to Europe, the Arab Palestinians practically gained control over the commercial system all over the country.[222] From 1937 to 1957, Arab merchants controlled 75 percent of investments in the import-export sector and about 50 percent of investments in manufacturing.[223] High levels of investment gave Palestinians and their descendants major control of manufacturing employment. By the 1960s, "Arab-controlled factories in San Pedro Sula and Tegucigalpa employed from 35% to 45% of Hondurans working in factory based manufacturing."[224] Recently, Palestinian entrepreneurs have extended their reach into the free-zone industries, and names such as Juan Canahuati, Gabriel Kattan, George Mitri, and Roberto Handal appear at the top of the list of investors in the free-zone sector of the economy.[225]

Many Palestinian businesses in Honduras, both commercial establishments and industrial plants, are still family-based businesses. In almost every single interview, there was a reference to a brother or an uncle who had established a business in Central America and asked his brother or nephew to join him to run the business.

El Salvador is another showcase of economic success by Palestinian immigrants. Early Palestinian immigrants spread throughout the country and established commercial and agricultural enterprises in the provinces of San Salvador, San Miguel, Santa Ana, and La Unión. Just like in Honduras, early Palestinian immigrants in El Salvador filled the socioeconomic gap created by the outdated attitudes toward commercial activities among the Salvadoran elite. The local aristocracy had a long history of disdain for local commercial activities, which were considered socially degrading and not fit for a "nobleman." For the Creole hidalgo, living off his hacienda (large estate) or large-scale commerce, any menial job or small business was degrading and dishonorable.[226]

Most of the Palestinian immigrants to El Salvador became apparel and shoes merchants. There are also successful Palestinian businessmen in the food-processing sector. The Safie Family, for example, bought the Gerber Company in El Salvador. The Salume family, which arrived in El Salvador in 1914, opened a chain of supermarkets, and more recently, the very prosperous company called Distribuidora Salum. The Simán family became one of the wealthiest families in El Salvador. They own several large and modern shopping centers in up-scale neighborhoods of San Salvador, and have recently extended their chain of shopping malls to other Central American countries including Nicaragua. Palestinians and their descendants in El Salvador are also very successful in the financial sector of the country and have extended their reach to other Central American financial markets. Isa Miguel, a descendant of a Palestinian immigrant to El Salvador, for example, owns about 40 percent of the Banco de la Vivienda, in Guatemala.[227] Some observers believe that the overwhelming majority of the estimated 90,000 Palestinian immigrants and their descendants in El Salvador belong to the top 5% of the economic scale.[228]

Discrimination

With the growing economic power of the Palestinian communities in the 1920s and 1930s, it was probably inevitable that the local elites would come to see them as economic rivals and try to isolate them socially and politically. Because Palestinian success was most visible in Honduras, the situation was especially acute there. As Dario Euraque observes, "Even in the 1940s and 1950s most Hondurans did not perceive the Arab immigrants as 'nationals,' regardless of their economic position and regardless of their official status as settled and/or naturalized Honduran citizens."[229] Palestinians were not welcome in important social clubs in San Pedro Sula and La Ceiba, such as Lodge EUREKA no. 2 (of Freemasons), Casino Sampedrano, and Hipodromo. All these clubs were open to North American and European immigrants,[230] but closed to Palestinians, even the rich and economically successful ones. According to many contemporary commentators, "Honduran officials had failed to administer immigration policy selectively, and instead of European immigration, Honduras received what Antonio Ochoa Alcántara called 'exotic' immigrants – Greeks, Chinese, and Palestinians who did not settle the land but rather limited their enterprise to stores and commercial operations in urban centers."[231]

The word turcos for Palestinian and other Arab immigrants, a misnomer arising from their Turkish (Ottoman) passports in the late nineteenth and early twentieth centuries, became a social slur used by Central Americans resentful of their economic success. The term is still used to this day as an insult in parts of Central and South America.

Fueling resentments was the tight-knit nature of the Palestinian community. Perceiving their situation in Central America as temporary and intending to return home after accumulating sufficient wealth, most early Palestinian immigrants married Palestinians or other Arabs. Their businesses were family-owned, and they did not mingle much with Central Americans economically or socially. Their isolation, combined with their success, made them an easy target. By 1922, the influential Honduran daily El Cronista was able to demand the expulsion of the "turcos" from San Pedro Sula and elsewhere in the north coast on the grounds that they were "harmful to the country."[232]

The onset of the Great Depression in 1929, which hit the export-oriented Central American economies hard, intensified the anti-immigrant sentiment, spawning the anti-immigration legislation, especially in Honduras and El Salvador. In Honduras, Article 8 of the new Regulations for Immigration Law of 2 September 1929 dictates that immigrants of "Arab, Turkish, Syrian, Armenian… [races] should bring a capital of five thousand silver pesos each, and make a deposit of five hundred silver pesos per person."[233] These laws were, at least partially, a response to complaints of the Honduran economic elite and their cultural agents, targeting the successful Palestinian merchant class. Even though the laws slowed the rate of new Palestinian immigration, anti-Palestinian voices continued to be raised. In the 1940s and 1950s, writings of middle-class Honduran intellectuals such as Antonio Ochoa Alcántara, Oscar A. Flores, and Adolfo Miranda helped inflame anti-Arab sentiments in the country. They criticized the government for its past liberal immigration laws and demanded additional tightening of immigration policies.[234]

El Salvador, like Honduras, was a showcase of economic success by Palestinian immigrants and had the second largest Palestinian community in Central America.[235] And as had been the case in Honduras, their commercial success made them targets for discrimination. In 1936, the repressive dictatorship of Maximiliano Hernández Martínez, who came to power in a 1931 military coup, passed Decree No. 49 (15 May 1936), the first of a series of discriminatory laws that forbade "persons of the Arab, Palestinian, Turkish, Chinese, Lebanese, Syrian, Egyptian, Persian, Hindu, and Armenian races, even though naturalized, to open new businesses of any type or even to participate in them as partners or to open branches of existing enterprises."[236] Article 40 of Decree No. 39 (24 July 1941) established a fine of 200 colons for officials of any municipality that permitted persons of the above races, regardless their nationality, to open or manage a commercial or industrial establishment."[237] It is important to emphasize that the laws included the immigrants' descendants born in El Salvador, as well as naturalized citizens.

In Guatemala, President Jorge Ubico (1931-1944) issued Decree No. 1813 on 4 May 1936, which forbade the opening of new commercial and industrial establishments, or branches of existing ones, "which are to be owned or directed by individuals of the following nationalities: Turks, Syrians, Lebanese, Arabs, Palestinians, Armenians, Egyptians, Persians, Afghans, Hindus, and Polish, as well as members of races originating in the African continent."[238]

While the discriminatory laws of Honduras, El Salvador, and Guatemala dated to the 1930s and 1940s, Costa Rica, which prides itself on a population claiming European ancestry, had long been determined to limit non-white immigration. In 1897, for example, the government prohibited the arrival of new Chinese immigrants,[239] and in 1904 enacted Decree No. 1 (10 June 1904) barring entry to anyone of Arab, Armenian, Turkish, or Gypsy origin, regardless of their nationality.[240] In 1930, another series of laws and regulations set additional limits on immigration and required foreign visitors to report their place of residence and activities to the government, although clauses allowed the authorities to exempt "honorable" [meaning white] foreigners from the regulations.[241] The restrictive immigration policies effectively prevented any significant Palestinian immigration to Costa Rica. In the early twentieth century, there were only two Palestinian immigrants in Costa Rica, Salvador Hasbun and Zacarías Bakit, both of whom had shops in Puerto Limón. Even as late as 1997, Roberto Marín Guzman could document only 22 Palestinian families in the country.[242] Although the community today is economically successful and well-integrated into Costa Rican society, heavy restrictions against any new immigration from Palestine and other Arab countries remain in place.[243]

An unintended consequence of the anti-immigration/anti-Palestinian discrimination and legislation of the 1930s was to hasten the assimilation of the Palestinian community in the host countries. In Honduras, where during the early decades few Palestinians had opted for Honduran citizenship, the number of naturalizations increased rapidly following the new law as a means of avoiding the legal obstacles it created.[244] In El Salvador, an additional consequence that was emphasized in interviews was the new tendency among Palestinians in the 1930s and 1940s to try to conceal their ethnic identity and refrain from speaking Arabic outside their homes as a result of incidents against Palestinian youth speaking Arabic in public. This was one reason for the loss of the Arabic language among children of the immigrants.[245] It is likely that the trend to marry outside the community was also hastened by the discrimination.

At present, descendants of early Palestinian immigrants are completely integrated into their host societies and are an important part of national life and social, political, and cultural institutions at all levels. Traditions such as intergroup marriages and concentrations of Palestinians in the same neighborhoods are few and far between. The price for Palestinians of full integration, however, has been the loss of their culture, especially the language and knowledge of their past. Today, the majority of Palestinian descendants marry non-Arabs; it is difficult to find Palestinian families without non-Palestinian members.[246] Most Palestinian descendants do not speak Arabic, although they might use some Arabic words and phrases.

Palestinians and Politics in Central America

An important indicator of the success of Palestinian integration/assimilation in Central America – and a striking reversal of the social rejection and discrimination they had previously suffered – is the political prominence that Palestinian descendants have achieved in the adopted countries in the last few decades. This is particularly the case in Honduras and El Salvador where the Palestinian communities are largest. Thus, in December 1997, Honduran voters elected Carlos Flores Facussé, the son of a Palestinian mother, to the highest office in the land; his five-year term ended in 2002. Honduras also counts at least 12 deputies of Palestinian descent in its 120-member parliament, and Palestinian descendants have served as vice-president (William Handal), president of the Central Bank (Victoria Asfoura), and minister-at-large (Juan Bendeck).[247] The current minister of foreign relations, Mario Miguel Canahuati, is also of Palestinian origin. In El Salvador, the grandson of Palestinian immigrants from Bethlehem, Elías Antonio Saca González, served as president from 2004 to 2009.

The majority of Palestinian immigrants and their descendants belong to the conservative current of Central American politics. In the region's sharp political divide, most wealthy business people, including Palestinian entrepreneurs, stand with the center-right political parties, which support the U.S. economic and political agenda in Central America. Former Honduran president Flores Facussé, for example, belonged to the center-right Liberal Party, while former Salvadoran president Saca was a leading member of right-wing Alianza Republicana Nacionalista (Nationalist Republican Alliance), or ARENA, which governed El Salvador from 1989 to 2009 on an extremely conservative political and economic platform.[248] As president, Antonio Saca continued his party's pro-U.S. policies and even supported Salvadoran participation in the U.S. war in Iraq.

On the other hand, Palestinian communities in Central America have also generated important figures of the Left long engaged in the struggle for social justice in the region. The best-known is El Salvador's Schafik Handal,[249] a Marxist and a former guerrilla commander, who was Antonio Saca's principal opponent in the 2004 presidential elections. Handal was the son of Palestinian immigrants from Bethlehem, but the politics of the two men could hardly be more different. Whereas Saca was an ardent anti-communist, Handal had close ties with Latin American revolutionary movements. In fact, the two men could be said to personally embody the Right/Left divide of Central American politics. Handal was instrumental in the 1980 formation of the Frente Farabundo Martí para la Liberación Nacional (Farabundo Martí National Liberation Front), or FMLN, an alliance of Salvadoran revolutionary organizations that fought the right-wing, U.S.-armed and funded, Salvadoran government and military establishment in a long and vicious civil war that claimed some 75,000 lives. After the government and the FMLN signed a peace accord in 1992 that ended the civil war, Handal transformed his guerrilla army into a political party, which is today El Salvador's leading party on the Left. He was elected to parliament as the head of the FMLN party bloc before running unsuccessfully for president against Saca in 2004. He died in 2006 of a heart attack while returning home from the inauguration of Bolivia's newly elected left-wing president, Evo Morales. Such was Handal's popularity in the country that President Saca was obliged to call three days of national mourning.[250] At his funeral, Handal's casket was wrapped in Salvadoran and Palestinian flags.[251]

Although the Handal family originated in the merchant class, many of its members have been active in the country's leftist political formations and progressive organizations. Schafik's brother, Antonio Handal, was one of the thousands who "disappeared" by the Salvadoran regime in the 1980s, and another brother, Farid Handal, head of the Salvadoran Communist Party, was killed in combat in 1989.[252] Schafik's son, Jorge Schafik Handal Vega, also an FMLN leader, has served as an FMLN deputy in the Central American parliament.[253]

In Nicaragua, as in other Central American countries, most of the Palestinian immigrants historically were on the conservative side of the political divide. Most were assimilated into Nicaraguan society and involved in commerce. In general, the community, which was small,[254] had established friendly relations with successive U.S.-supported Nicaraguan governments, including those of Anastasio Somoza García, who took power in 1936, and his son, Anastasio Somoza Debayle, who continued the family dictatorship that spawned the Sandinista revolution that triumphed in 1979. As immigrants, most Palestinians feared the regime and were concerned about losing their businesses or even being deported if identified as political opponents. Some were so close to the Somoza ruling circle that they had to leave the country following the Sandinista victory. Federico Frech, for example, was accused of being a member of Somoza's Office of National Security. Also, properties of several wealthy Palestinian-Nicaraguans, including Mario Salha and Ali Khalil, were confiscated by the revolutionary government because of their ties to Somoza and his National Guard.[255]

As Moisés Hassan observed, the "majority of Palestinian immigrants were not supportive of the revolution because a lot of them did not identify themselves as Nicaraguan. For them, Nicaragua was a place where they lived and worked but did not have that much interest in national affairs. The only interest they had was that the government let them work. They were afraid if they said anything against Somoza, he would deport them from the country, or hurt their businesses. So the majority of them were very conservative. But the young Palestinians were in a different position. They identified as Nicaraguans and had a lot of nationalist sentiment about the country. They also were very sensitive about the situation in Palestine."[256]

A number of young Palestinian-Nicaraguans joined the Frente Sandinista de Liberación Nacional (Sandinista National Liberation Front), or FSLN, in the 1970s, and some died fighting for the cause, including Selim Shible, Omar Hassan, Amín Halum, Mauricio Abdalah, and Soraya Hassan.[257] Some of the Palestinian descendants who joined the revolutionary struggle were appointed to top positions in the revolutionary government in the 1980s, including Moisés Hassan, a member of the first revolutionary government, the National Directorate, and Suad Marcos Frech, a famous Nicaraguan poet, who had joined the Sandinistas at a very young age and became an officer in the Sandinista Army. Later, in the 1980s, she held a top position in the Interior Ministry. In the immediate wake of the triumph of the Nicaraguan revolution in 1979, Suad Marcos went to Beirut to join the Palestinian movement and remained there with the leadership of the PLO during Israel's 1982 invasion of the country.[258]

In fact, soon after the Sandinista victory, the PLO opened an embassy in Managua, and Yasser Arafat visited the country for the first anniversary of the revolution. The Palestinian Embassy in Nicaragua today is the only one in Central America.

National Identity

The process of social, political, and cultural assimilation for the Central American Palestinian communities was slow and often painful. Even today, although Palestinian descendants born in Central America identify themselves as citizens of these countries, most of them refer to Palestine as their roots.

The anti-immigration laws of the 1930s virtually halted Palestinian immigration to Central America for some years. But the 1948 Nakba that accompanied Israel's creation spawned over 700,000 Palestinian refugees, some of whom sought to join relatives and friends in Central America. Israel's 1967 occupation of the West Bank and Gaza Strip created another wave of refugees, some of whom went to Central America. In recent years, the flow of immigration directly from Palestine has intensified because of the worsening economic and political conditions in the occupied territories.[259]

Since their arrival in Honduras, the Palestinian immigrants have created organizations and associations for the community to preserve their cultural heritage, keep the community informed of the events in Palestine, and organize acts of solidarity with the Palestinian people. In San Pedro Sula, for example, as early as the 1930s, the Palestinian community formed an organization called Union Palestina. A few years later the Palestinian community in Tegucigalpa established Sociedad Union Juventud Árabe (Arab Youth Union Society), which later created similar entities in Mexico, Cuba, Guatemala, El Salvador, and Nicaragua. It published a weekly paper called "Rumbo" and began a radio program called "La hora árabe" transmitted by the Honduran National Radio.[260]

To preserve their religious and national heritage, the Palestinian community in San Pedro Sula established the first Orthodox Church in 1963, which became a major focus of the community. The Church later founded several predominantly Palestinian organizations, including the Comite Ortodoxo, the Comite de Damas Ortodoxas, and the Club Juvenil. In addition to these Church-related organizations, there is a Palestinian Sports Club (Club Deportivo Palestino), the Associación Femenina Hondurena Árabe, the Centro Cultural Árabe, and FEARAB (Federación de Entidades Americano-Árabe). FEARAB is known for its political activities.[261]

The Orthodox Church has also been involved in the political defense of Palestinians in the occupied territories, organizing special masses to commemorate the Palestinian victims of the Intifada, and has published paid statements in local papers in solidarity with Palestinians.[262]

Palestinian immigrants in El Salvador also tried to preserve their cultural heritage by creating organizations for the community. One of these organizations was the Club Palestino, which later was renamed Club El Prado. The organization gradually changed to a social club with a few elements of Arab culture, such as music and dance.[263] Most of the descendants of Palestinian immigrants in El Salvador are completely assimilated in the local society and consider themselves Salvadorans. They do not speak Arabic and have not preserved Palestinian culture. In spite of their identification with El Salvador, some of the Palestinian descendants demonstrate a high degree of sensitivity toward and solidarity with the struggle of Palestinian people. In San Salvador, for example, the descendants of Palestinian immigrants have funded the construction of two monuments in solidarity with the Palestinian struggle. Interviews with Palestinian descendants in Central American countries repeatedly pointed to a growing feeling of pride in the Palestinian heritage among the younger generation and a deep sense of sadness and anger about the events in Palestine.[264] Solidarity with Palestinian people is the common political ground among the community, which is otherwise deeply divided on political issues.

The arrival of new Palestinian immigrants from the homeland has created a continuous connection between Central America and Palestine. The newcomers, both Christian and Muslim, brought with them experiences of a suffering people under military occupation, which reinforced the older community's sense of connection with Palestine. According to anthropologist Nancie Gonzalez, "with every crisis between Arabs and Jews in Israel and the occupied territories, new emigrants arrive in Honduras, where their stories are avidly sought and repeated throughout the Palestinian community, both in San Pedro and elsewhere in the country."[265] Political symbols of an independent Palestine, such as the Palestinian flag and resistance songs, have become popular among the early immigrants and their descendants in Central America, and solidarity with the struggle of the Palestinian people is on the rise in the region's diaspora communities.

The new arrivals, while trying to integrate into their host societies, are more motivated to preserve their Palestinian identity than earlier immigrants, probably because of the politicization and development of national identity that accompanies life under occupation or in the refugee camps. They do not see themselves as voluntary immigrants but as exiles, and, as such, are far more active in solidarity politics and the preservation of their culture as acts affirming their national identity.

Many of the new immigrants, especially after the 1967 war, are Muslim, and they have been particularly active in building community networks and organizing gatherings to celebrate and preserve national and religious events. The early Muslim Palestinian immigrants to Central America were unsuccessful in building their communities and preserving their culture and religion for reasons discussed earlier in this chapter. There was no mosque in Central America for Muslim Palestinians to continue their religious practices as a community or to teach their children the tenets of their religious beliefs. The situation changed when Muslim Palestinians began arriving in Central America following the 1967 war. The newcomers established mosques and have made efforts to teach their children Arabic and Islamic doctrine. Since most came directly from the occupied territories or from the refugee camps in Lebanon, Syria, or Jordan, they kept in close contact with their relatives in the region, often maintaining secondary residences in the Middle East. It is not uncommon for Palestinian immigrants, especially Muslims, to send their children back to Palestine or to neighboring countries, such as Jordan, to attend school and learn Arabic and Islamic doctrine.[266]

For example, Muslims, who predominated in the post-1967 Palestinian immigration to Costa Rica, today constitute a prominent community in the country. They are highly educated professionals, enjoying wide respect in the country, and they have been active in preserving their cultural and religious heritage, partly through the Asociación Cultural Islámica de Costa

Rica (Islamic Cultural Association of Costa Rica), founded in 1994 by Dr. Abd al-Fattah Sa'sa, a Palestinian refugee from a camp in Jordan who arrived in 1973.[267] Despite their small number, Costa Rica's Palestinian community is active in educating the local population on the situation in Palestine, organizing academic conferences and seminars at local universities and sponsoring political debates and radio programs on Palestine.[268] The Palestinian community reportedly played a role in encouraging President Oscar Arias to move the Costa Rican Embassy from Jerusalem to Tel Aviv in the summer of 2006.[269] Ten days later, El Salvador's President Saca followed suit, marking a diplomatic setback for Israel: Costa Rica and El Salvador had been the last two countries in the world maintaining embassies in Jerusalem, and their presence there had constituted recognition of Jerusalem as Israel's capital, denied by the United Nations and other countries, including the United States, since 1948.

The new immigrants' commitment to the Palestinian struggle has injected new energy in the Palestinian communities in Central America. Everywhere in the region, solidarity with the Palestinian people has become the common political ground among immigrant communities, which are otherwise deeply divided on political issues. The construction of the Plaza Palestina in San Salvador in 2004 – just before the presidential elections that pitted two men of Palestinian origin, Antonio Saca and Schafik Handal, against each other – is a case in point. Although they belonged to the two extremes of the Salvadoran politics, both men supported and contributed to the Plaza. The commemorative plaque, which honors the "victims of Israel's creation in 1948" and features a map of pre-partition Palestine, bears their names as donors. This is another demonstration of the unity of Palestinian-Salvadorans on the issue of Palestine, although they belong to different, and often opposing, political factions in national politics.[270] In 2005, Handal's FMLN party was responsible for a second memorial park in San Salvador, dedicated to the late Yaser Arafat. Plaza Arafat caused a diplomatic dispute, which resulted in Israel's withdrawing of its ambassador to El Salvador.[271]

Conclusion:

Palestinian emigration to Central America came in two waves: the first, arriving in the early decades of the twentieth century, and the second in its later half. The first came as temporary emigrants were seeking economic opportunities but ultimately decided to settle, while the second came after the loss of their homeland when the Israeli state was created, and therefore knew from the beginning that theirs would be a permanent diaspora. The first passed through a difficult process of adjustment in their adopted countries stemming from cultural differences and an early resistance to social integration, and had to weather a long period of prejudice and discrimination fueled by their economic success. By the time the second wave began to arrive in substantial numbers (mainly after 1967), the descendants of the Palestinians of the first wave had already achieved full assimilation and the highest degree of economic, social, and political success. But the more recent flow of immigrants made an important contribution to the established community; they reconnected it to Palestine and awakened it to the Palestinian national identity that had been emerging.

Today, most Palestinian descendants born in Central America, whether part of the earlier wave of immigration or the later one, identify themselves as citizens of their adopted countries. But as Gonzalez observed, "the additional Palestinian identification has never ceased to be important."[272] John Nasser Hasbun, a Palestinian-Salvadoran and a member of the San Salvador City Council in 2007, explained his identity by saying, "I am proud to be Salvadoran, but I am also proud to be Palestinian."[273]

A Century of Palestinian Immigration to Chile: A Successful Integration

Nicole Saffie Guevara and Lorenzo Agar Corbinos

Thousands of Arabs in the late nineteenth and early twentieth centuries decided to leave their homeland in hope to find a better future. This was motivated by the persecution set forth by the Turkish Ottoman Empire, which recruited young Christians in their ranks to fight on the battlefront. Added to this were the poor living conditions and lack of opportunities for Christians who, according to the prevailing law, were not allowed to serve in public office. Having been considered a constitutive and privileged minority, this allowed them to live relatively better, and yet this status was also frowned upon by their Muslim neighbors. All of these factors led many Christians to undertake the long journey to an uncertain fate that could be as promising as America: a continent which, at that time, was a preferred destination for thousands of European immigrants who arrived thanks to the settlement acts a matter that did not favor the Palestinian immigrants.

Despite their eagerness to start a new life, the Arabs who were leaving their homeland did not know exactly what to expect in these distant lands. This notion is manifested in this small fragment from the novel "The Turks":

- *Tell me Hannah, will you go far with me?*
- *Far? Where?*
- *To America.*
- *America?*
- *Yes, like the son of the baker Yuma. He has writen to his brother and says he has made a fortune* [274]

In the case of the Palestinians in Haifa and Jaffa, the adventure began when they boarded a boat carrying them to a European port, which was usually Genoa or Marseilles, and that was where they had their first contact with Western culture. It could be weeks or even months before they were able to buy a ticket to the much-coveted American continent, with little or no care as to where exactly they would arrive. The important thing was to get on board.

The journey was hard. The migrants had to buy a third-class passenger ticket or board cargo ships, where they were accommodated in between luggage. Despite the precariousness of the journey, however, this time allowed them to establish contacts and obtain useful information on their destination. New York in the U.S. and Santos in Brazil were the two ports where most of the passengers disembarked, although some continued south to the last stop of the continent: Buenos Aires, Argentina's capital.

One account of this long journey is told by Kamel Jarufe Jadue, who emigrated to America from Beit Jala:

> *We first went to Lebanon to take the boat. We slept a night there. We boarded the boat, but not the one we had to make for the long trip, this boat was small, it was Turkish, and it went to Greece. There we took the other ship, it was gigantic, it was called "Bretain," it was an Italian ship, it was immense. The first couple of days we could not eat anything, we were all seasick. The first port we came to was Marseille, there we stayed about five days, then to Barcelona, Spain. Spain is beautiful, everything changes, even the color of the people, customs, language, people are more loving, not like the Italians or the French. There were few Palestinians on the boat, and from our town it was just us. After Spain, we arrived to Dakar, in the north of Africa, there, they are all black. In Palestine we had never seen a black man. In Dakar, we stayed one more day, then on to Brazil. The boat stopped in Santos, a very old city. We slept a night there. Then we went to Rio de Janeiro, just in time for Carnival. I had never seen these things before, I was amazed, the music is different; my music is soft, you feel it. From Rio de Janeiro we continued to Buenos Aires, it took five days. That completed the 45-day trip, with stops included .[275]*

There was a daring group of travelers who decided to go to the end of the world: Chile. That crossing was a challenge. It began in the city of Mendoza, Argentina, in the foothills of the Andes, where the adventurers had to wait for the weather to settle down before crossing the mountains. Then they undertook the journey on mules, challenging for about four days dangerous cliffs and the cold Andean mountain range in order to reach the city of Los Andes on Chilean soil. Only in 1908 did the railroad come to the mountain range of Puente del Inca and in 1912, to the station of Las Cuevas, and down to the Chilean station, Caracoles. From there, the passengers continued on mules to Juncal, where they boarded the Chilean Trans-Andean train .[276]

This group was the first to do that in the second half of the nineteenth century. There is no certainty about the origin or identity of those that crossed in the second half of the nineteenth century. In the 1854 census, two people are identified as "Turks." Then, in 1865 and 1875 three more are also referred to as "Turks." Only in 1881 was there a record of the first Palestinian. Four years later, 29 Arabs were recorded. The first travelers with known identities were Abraham Saffe, a Syrian, and Santiago Beirutí, a Lebanese, who arrived in 1888. Between 1905 and 1914 Palestinian immigrants reached 56%. By 1920, there have been a lot of immigrants of Arab origin, distributed as follows: 1,164 Palestinians, 1,204 Syrians, 15 Lebanese, 1,282 Turkish and 1,849 "Arabs."[277] In 1941, the Social Guide to the Arab community had a total of 2,994 Arab families, approximately 15,000 people, of whom 85% were immigrants and 15% were their first offspring born on Chilean soil. Half of them were of Palestinian origin.

The First Years in Chile

In the early twentieth century, Chile offered good economic conditions, mostly due to the nitrate boom in the northern territory. However, the policies had already been completed in support of migrants and were especially favoring the Germans, who were offered land to colonize the south. The Palestinians did not meet the requirements given forth by the Chilean State. They had no profession or money, and had to fend for themselves, which they did quite successfully. As an immigrant recounts, "when leaving their homes to a place where they knew nor the language or customs, and could hardly even pronounce its name, they faced a huge challenge."[278]

These were usually young single men. According to the Social Guide, 40.2% of Arab immigrants who arrived to Chile were 10-19 years old, while 26.7% were 20-30. In other words, over 60% were younger than 30 years old. Men accounted for 76.6% of all immigrants, with a total of 2,656 persons in 1940. Women, meanwhile, came as dependents, either as wives or daughters, and were a much smaller number; only 495 for the same date, equivalent to 14.2% of the total.

Most came from the same places. Beit Jala and Bethlehem were the towns that contributed the most to the migration population, with 18% and 17% respectively. Palestinian immigrants that came from Beit Jala were 35.7%, and from Bethlehem, 34.6%.[279] The remainder came from Beit Sahour and Beit Safafa, within the limits of Jerusalem. Immigrants tended to settle in the cities or neighborhoods where they had relatives, acquaintances, or members of their own town. They had a fundamental role to play as they helped find places to live; they found jobs and passed on some basic cultural information of their new homeland. They even taught them their first words in Spanish.

> *The first young people who came to Chile told their family and friends who remained in Palestine, that this was a blessed land of opportunities and possibilities. They talked about good people comparing them to Arabs, a pleasant climate, delicious fruits and many employment opportunities. This image was transmitted from one family to another and by word of mouth which helped and encouraged young people to do the same, increasing the number of Palestinian immigrants*[280]

The great amount of Palestinians settled in provinces, like Ovalle in the north, San Felipe, La Calera, and Curicó in the central zone, and Chillán, Concepción, and Los Ángeles in the south. This phenomenon is known as "chain migration." The territorial spread was characteristic of the Arabs, unlike other immigrant groups like the Jews, who concentrated more in the capital. In 1940, 62% (1,866 families) of the total Arab population settled in different locations in Chile, preferring secondary cities than major urban centers. Only 36% of Palestinian families settled in Santiago.[281]

The main profession of the Palestinians, like the Syrians and Lebanese, was trade. The "falte" (door-to-door salesman) or street vendor, who traveled the countryside on foot or by wagon, was the typical image selling a series of household items. The name comes from the phrase they repeated over and over again, often in mispronounced Spanish, "¿hay algo que le falte?" (Is there something you need?).[282]

As written by Olguín and Peña in "The Arab Immigration to Chile":
> *With their baskets overflowing with the most heterogeneous goods —scarves, socks, mirrors, pins, spools of thread, soap, buttons and combs— they constituted a figure too picturesque to pass unnoticed. They roamed the streets shouting their products in rudimentary Spanish with the familiar cry of "store thing", that is, things in a store.*[283]

But these individuals not only fulfilled a purely commercial role. As Allél writes:
> *(...) On those routes they carried more than just their various products. They carried with them civilization and progress, indirectly helping raise the social status of the inhabitants of those remote regions. They were the link between progress and ignorance.*[284]

Those who brought some resources or managed to collect enough money would set up their own shop. The Palestinians, like the rest of the Arab merchants, quickly gained fame. Many stores sold everything from food, toiletries, and household items to even farming tools. In Santiago, most of the Arab population living there in 1940 worked in trade and commerce: 49% were in "various branches of commerce", 18% in "stores and packaging", and 19% in "factories".[285]

Their work style contrasted with that of the average Chilean. They would open their doors early and close late at night. Hard work, a sense of responsibility and perseverance, are values that remain important in the Palestinian families to date.[286] Their life was simple and limited to spending only what was necessary. "Their expenses were low: rent and food. The thought of buying clothes and other extras was unthinkable. They didn't spend on anything that they could make themselves."[287] They were also described as "(...) austere, with high morals, respectful of the law, and hard working (...)."[288]

Many times they lived above or at the back of their business stores. The newcomers settled in very precarious housing. "They lived in the rooms in "cités" (houses shared by many families); there were four, six, or even more to a room. If the room was not in use, it became the kitchen." [289]

Many came looking to make money and then return home. However, the vast majority ended up settling for good in the country, as one Palestinian immigrant recounts:

> *Young people who came only intended to stay two or three years in this country. This was enough time to collect a few pounds to help the household finances back home. To the newcomer, none even sounded set on staying in this land of mystery nor be buried in it, unless those who, years later, came to meet with their children or grandchildren. Instead of returning to their countries, the immigrants, almost without noticing, were practically living in Chile; again and again extending their stay because they had found a place to work and progress. So instead of leaving, they brought their parents, siblings, even grandparents. Almost all formed their own families in the new homeland.*[290]

So, those who met with hard work and minimal expenses managed to bring their families. One by one they arrived, parents and siblings, wives and children, all of whom were then integrated to life in the new country. The newly arrived countrymen were also welcomed until they could go their own way.

According to census data, the total Arab population that arrived to Chile between 1885 and 1940 ranged between 8,000 and 10,000. In the 1930 census, the largest number of Arab immigrants was registered: 6,703.[291]

Sundus Nasser affirms:

> *In Beit Jala, Bethlehem, and Beit Sahour they know more about Chile than the common Chilean knows about the Middle East. Almost every family in these three cities has a family member that immigrated to Chile, cousins, nephews, grandchildren, siblings, aunts, uncles or friends. Most Palestinian Christians are in Chile.*[292]

Immigration began to decline in the 1930s due to improved living conditions in Palestine after the fall of the Turkish Empire and the establishment of British rule. However, with the declaration of the State of Israel in 1948 and the subsequent forced migration of Palestinians from their land, there was a small wave of immigration to Chile, although the vast majority remained as refugees in neighboring countries like Jordan, Syria, and Lebanon. A similar phenomenon occurred in 1967 because of the Six Day War.

Since then, Palestinian immigration to the country has been rather sporadic. The exception was the immigration of 117 Palestinian refugees from the al-Tanf camp on the border of Iraq and Syria in 2008. However, this was a Muslim group.[293]

The First Steps Toward Integration

Without knowing much of the language and customs of the host society, in the beginning, the Palestinians gathered in the same neighborhoods and villages. They helped each other and married one another, replicating life of their native land, with the same values and social codes. However, as migrants set up in Chile and brought their families, they increasingly integrated into the country thanks to trade relations, shared beliefs, and Christian values.

The new generations accelerated the integration. Through education, wealth, mixed marriage, and the settling to various sectors of Santiago and the country in general, they became part of Chilean society. Today, their contribution can be seen in the most varied fields of economic, political, social, and cultural affairs.

The following section will analyze the different aspects that show the integration of the Palestinian community in the country by: religion, commerce, marriage, media, and geographic location.

• *Religion*

The key element that the Palestinians and Chilean immigrants shared was religion. In the late nineteenth and early twentieth centuries, it was estimated that almost all the inhabitants of Bethlehem and Beit Jala, where most of the Palestinian immigrants came from, were Christian Orthodox. Thus, the newcomers shared the same values and religious beliefs like most Catholics who lived and to this day continue to live in the country. Moreover, many decided to change to the Roman Catholic Rite.

It is possible that one of the reasons for this change was the lack of churches of worship. The first Orthodox priest who arrived in Chile was Father Paul Jury in 1910 from Syria. In 1914, during a visit to Latin America, Elias Dib, Archbishop of Tyre and Sidon (Margeyioun Nazareth, south of Lebanon), ordained Yuri Solomon, a native of Beit Jala. Only on 24 October 1917 did the first Orthodox Patriarchate of Antioch Church open St. George's Cathedral in Chile, in honor of a saint revered for centuries by Arab Christians. In a Byzantine style and with typical spatial characteristics of the Orthodox churches in the Middle East, it was situated in Patronato, an emblematic neighborhood of Arab immigrants, which then converted itself into the main hub for the community.

But probably the main motivation for this change in Palestinian immigrants was to join their newfound country and establish new relationships with Chile, which also favored mixed marriages. According to a survey conducted in 2001 by Daniela Lahsen, of 306 Palestinian families from Beit Jala, 72% of first immigrants were Orthodox and 28% were Roman Catholic. However, with the second generation, born in Chile, this relationship reversed and was now 70% Roman Catholic and only 30% Orthodox. The Encuesta a Población de Origen Árabe (Arabic Origins Community Survey), EPOA 2001, confirmed the phenomenon: 69% of respondents claimed to be Catholic and only 14% Orthodox.[294] Moreover, a survey of students at the Arabic School of Santiago in 2006, which included young people between the ages of 16 and 18 of Arab origin, confirmed the difference, but in another ratio: 46.5% were Catholic and 34.9% Orthodox. There was also one Muslim student counted.[295]

Currently, it is important to mention that the largest Palestinian Christian community in the world is in Chile.

• *Trade*

Trade allowed the Palestinian immigrants to quickly establish relationships with the Chileans and to learn the language and aspects of their culture. It was also an important factor to move away from the capital and settle in the provinces, traveling to rural areas with their goods, settling in cities and small towns.

The entrepreneurial spirit of the Palestinians led them to make major contributions to the Chilean economy. It was the Arab immigrants and their descendants who helped found many of the companies in this country. Allél (1937) realized the contribution of Palestinian, Syrian, and Lebanese businessmen in the country. He says:

> *Following tradition, members of these conglomerates dedicated themselves to trade. Their ignorance of the language was not a problem for the normal development of their daily activities, and despite the fundamental difference between their customs and those of the country, they adapted quickly, as if they were in their own homeland.*[296]

> *(...) The members of the Arab family, from their arrival to Chile, played an important role in business development; and in this country, it was in need of a strong push. These men contributed greatly and devoted all their strength*

to conquer a place that allowed them to develop their high ingenious and progressive aspirations.[297]

According to this author, the first immigrants to establish their own companies were the Schain Brothers, in perfumery, and Abdala Manzur, in the manufacturing of leather articles, in 1910. However, it was only in the following decade when the Palestinians dared to take the plunge and began to establish businesses in greater numbers. The pioneers were the Hirmas, Valech, and Cadi families in hosiery, and Hasbún in the manufacturing of silk.[298]

Textile was undoubtedly the main industry in which the first immigrants flourished and advanced. In just 15 years, 80% of the textile and spinning mills in Chile were owned by people of Arab origin. In 1937, the opening of the formidable spinning mill of the Palestinian Yarur Brothers took place, "which is the most outstanding and superb exponent of the progressive spirit of the Arab race. It immediately placed this national industry above their South American counterparts."[299]

However, the Arabs ventured into almost all areas of the national economy: agriculture, livestock, mining, chemicals and pharmaceuticals, services, and much more. In the first half of the twentieth century, the Schain Brothers soap and perfume factories appeared; as did the Distillery Spirits of Chile S.A. of the Toumani and Nacrur families; the thermo-plastics factory of Emilio Yazig, Fred Haleby, and Fadul Mehech; Talcon Minerals "San Carlos de Corral" of Jorge Chamy; manufacturing of rubber articles of Salomón Saffie; combs and toothbrushes manufacturing company of Schain, Betinyani and Namur; and Karmy Brothers Jewelry, among others.

By 1941, according to the Social Guide, most people of Arab origin worked in the commercial sector (823 surveyed), meanwhile the professionals represented a very minor number (108). According to Allél, Arab industries were allowed to hire between 9,000 to 10,000 workers, a significant labor force for the time when unemployment soared in the country and the economic crisis of the 1930s had left its mark. The state also contributed directly through taxes and increased domestic consumption, encouraging domestic investment.

The entrepreneurial spirit was transmitted to new generations that followed the path of their parents in setting up new businesses and enterprises. However, the textile industry was no longer the dominant trade, as they were moving into other areas according to their own studies and interests. In the early 1980s, 23% of all companies engaged in clothing manufacturing had an owner of Arab origin, while the category, specifically textile, rose to 48%. However, in 2000, the Arab population increased its stake to 33% in the clothing apparel field, but decreased to 36% in textiles.[300]

Currently, Palestinian surnames are among the wealthiest in the country: Said, linked to retail and banking; Sahié, owner of one of the largest newspaper in the country, along with retail and financial services; Abumohor, in banking, textile, agricultural, and real estate; Kassis, in food processing, and Yarur, linked to the banking sector, among many others.

• *Marriage*

Marriage is a good indicator that shows the level of integration of a community. At first, the Palestinians who arrived in the first half of the twentieth century as well as their children married people of their own community. The couples were predominantly "endogamic." The Palestinians, (and Arabs in general,) saw the Chilean women as very liberal, with "relaxed" habits especially in poor neighborhoods. As explained by Olguín and Peña:

> The first immigrants experienced a strong culture shock to see a new relationship between the sexes. While Chilean men and women kept unequal power within the relationship, the immigrants perceived the behavior of the women from the poor sectors as very different to that of the Arab woman. The distrust felt by the Arab men towards Chileans was because, in these sectors, the women were more "liberal" than they were used to.[301]

The idea of marrying a person who did not share the same values and culture and, in fact, who was not of the same community, was unthinkable. Thus, when the men were of marrying age, they sought out a partner within their own community. Those who had the resources to make the long journey back to their homeland traveled with the sole purpose of finding a wife. In other cases, efforts were made with the families of their hometown, who sent their daughters to marry a suitor installed in America.

Olguín and Peña describe this process very well:

> In its early days, the Arab man tended to marry within the same community, and who for various reasons did not relate to the Chileans: they had little command of the language, mutual distrust and perhaps most importantly because they couldn't conceive the idea of marrying anyone other than from their homeland, even more, from outside their own village and whose family they knew(...). At family councils, they proposed the likely candidates to the young men. In the case that they did not accept any, meant little options for finding others... One of them was to attend the activities of the Arab community, where boys and girls of a marriageable age attended. Another custom that spread throughout America was one in which deserving young men of age went to the ports where ships carrying Arab families disembarked. Among the offspring, one could find a future mate. When none of these ways worked, there was the last option of travelling to the homeland in search of a wife.[302]

Between 1910 and 1919, 88.4% of spouses were of Arab origin. Between 1920 and 1929, the phenomenon decreased, but slightly, to 83.7%. The reasoning behind this was probably the desire to preserve the deeply embedded traditions and roots.

However, the new generation that was born in Chile and more integrated into the society began to marry Chileans, initiating a process of mixed marriages that increased over time. This was due to the decline of Arab immigration into the country and to a growing acceptance of Chilean society and customs. In addition, the idea of returning to Palestine began to either fade or simply was not in the minds of the children born in this country, because many embraced their early years of life in Chile.

Between 1960 and 1969, the number of marriages between people of Arab origin fell to 47%, while the marriages with Chileans reached a significant 53%.[303] The EPOA survey [304] shows how this phenomenon has evolved. Respondents (137 people of Arab origin, of which 62 are descendants of Palestinians), were divided into three groups: businessmen, academics, and students. When asked about the origin of their parents, only 14% of businessmen had a parent whose origin was not Arab. However, among the academics this percentage increased to 47%, and amid the students, the majority of which are second or third generation, rose to 72%. This illustrates the gradual increase of mixed marriages in the new generations born in Chile. On the other hand, it also shows that those in business, for more endogenous economic reasons, tend to marry within the same origin.

Palestinians tend to marry within their own community. The same EPOA survey [305] shows that 62% of Palestinian respondents have both parents of the same origin, whereas in the case of the Syrians, those who have parents that share the same origin decreases to 50%. According to the survey conducted at the Arabic School in 2006, 90% of surveyed youth have parents of Arab origin, and in 60% of the cases the mother is of the same origin. Just over half have both parents of Arab origin.[306]

One can see here an increased integration of Palestinians and Arabs in general in the Chilean society. At the same time, however, there is still interest in maintaining and safeguarding their identity, as well as in preserving the values and customs handed down from generation to generation. That is to say, the paradox of our globalized world is on the one hand, to share as a whole, but on the other, to differentiate oneself from another. This was the case for those with Arab roots.

• *Media*

Shortly after installing themselves in the new world, the first immigrants created their own media to maintain a sense of community and strengthen cohesion. Its use was with the purpose to find out about new marriages, births, new arrivals, and various events to promote their products and services, and to express their own views on the most diverse events. As Ruiz and Saiz explained, "the Arabs in Chile seem concerned about protecting their cultural identity, linguistic, and religious diversity in a society still unknown that they perceived as hostile, whose language and customs were totally strange."[307]

The list of newspapers and magazines was quite considerable. The first was al-Murchid (The Guide), founded in 1912 in Santiago by Father Paul Jury. It was written entirely in Arabic and was funded by Jorge Hirmas, an immigrant born in Bethlehem who managed to become a successful businessman in Chile. Although the idea was to have a weekly issue, they accomplished to print, although in an irregular manner, over the following five years. His goal was to create an Arabic publication in the country to advertise the business community and to discuss events and news on the homeland from their perspective while also working as a link for the Christian Arab Orthodox community. When it came out, it only had two hundred subscriptions, but it served as a model for other papers that came later. Between 1944 and 1950 it reappeared as a bi-monthly magazine under the direction of Juan Zalaquett, a businessman and writer born in Lebanon, with a strong nationalist tinge. Although the first attempt was published in Arabic, Spanish increasingly gained ground.

Additionally, the magazine al-'Awatif (Feelings) was created in 1916 by Antonio Yamal, a Syrian-born businessman, and was published in the capital. The same year in Concepción, the newspaper al-Munir (The Torch) was released by Louis Sa'd. There was also al-Chabiba (The Youth, 1918) of Yamil Subhi, and al-Watan (The Nation, 1920) and al-Islah (The Reform, 1930). Oriente (The East, 1927) founded by Solomón Ahués, and Mundo Árabe (Arab World, 1935) from Jorge Sabaj, were both written entirely in Spanish. As Mercedes del Amo writes in her article, The Literature of the Arab Newspapers in Chile, these texts are "an invaluable source of written historical chronicle, wherein values are recorded, lifestyles, customs, concerns, nostalgias and how to relate with the new Arabic media."[308]

One of the longest-running and influential Arabic newspapers in the community was al-Watan, founded and led by Palestinian Issa Khalil Daccarett. Although economic issues had appeared since the beginning, the publication circulated for nine years. Arabic was its dominant language, but there were some sections in Spanish. The contents were political, social, and cultural, but after selling to Father Jury, the news and religious articles increased.

Another influential newspaper was the weekly al-Islah, owned by Jorge Sabaj, which ran for twelve years, from 1930-1942. Sabaj defined it as a social, cultural, and literary media, although it focused on the Palestinian conflict and the European settlement in the area. It was separated into two parts, one in Arabic and one in Spanish. Mercedes del Amo explains, "although the increase in space devoted to the Arabic language may seem contradictory due to loss of knowledge of the language by a large proportion of the immigrant population, the fact is that it was precisely this fear that led us to pay attention to the preservation of the native tongue."[309]

As stated by Ruiz and Saiz, with respect to the Arab press published in the first half of the twentieth century in Chile:

> *"Some of these newspapers opt for the dissemination of religious principles and teaching Arabic. Sometimes they combine these functions with those political and ideological, with international news, local information, social and of course, also cultural and literary activities."*[310]

There are still some newspapers in circulation, created and written by the descendants of the first, second, and even third generations born in Chile. The first is Mundo Árabe, founded by Jorge Sabaj Zurob in 1931 and taken up today by Elías Sabaj Chamy. There is also the magazine al-Damir (The Conscience), a publication of the Palestinian Bethlehem 2000 Foundation, founded in 2001. Both are written in Spanish and seek to keep the spirit of community alive for the new generations.

Although at first the newspapers and magazines were published entirely in Arabic, Spanish gradually took over more and more pages until it became the predominant language. This tells us a lot about the integration of new generations. In general, immigrants did not teach their language to their children, so they would learn Spanish as their native tongue, thereby avoiding some forms of discrimination due to the misuse of the language that they had suffered when they were new immigrants. They basically wanted their descendants to not be regarded as foreigners but as "genuine" Chileans.

• *Geographic Location*

At first, those of the Palestinian immigrants that settled in Santiago did so in poor areas such as Recoleta, San Pablo, and San Diego. The Palestinians were localized mainly in Recoleta (37%), being the migrating group that showed the highest concentration in a specific neighborhood of the capital. The immigrants and their descendants identified themselves with these neighborhoods because of its strong presence in the area.[311]

This occurred especially in the emblematic sector of Patronato, the poor outer boundary area of Santiago in the mid-twentieth century and is now the central business district of the middle-income class, where many Palestinian merchants settled into. Stores quickly surfaced, especially clothing and textile workshops. Kamel Jadue Jarufe recalls the beginnings of the Arab settlement in this part of the city:

> *When I arrived from Palestine, there were only six stores in the neighborhood, those stores were mostly paisanos [slang for Arab people] who came from Palestine. Then little by little they began to arrive, many from Bolivia. When one tells another that the neighborhood is good for business, they start to*

arrive. That's how this neighborhood came about. Everyone knew each other because this guy is married to the sister of that guy, another guy with another sister, etc... and so they began to bring their people. At that time there were many who were in Calera, Quillota, and San Javier (outside Santiago); but these places had deteriorated in terms of trade, so, those in Santiago began to bring their families from the outside towns.[312]

As the Palestinians began to increase their income thanks to factories, clothing manufacturing, and trade, they were settling in more affluent neighborhoods, such as Ñuñoa and Las Condes. "Although there was a majority presence in the center of Santiago, the trend was to abandon the poorer sectors in which the first immigrants dwelt and move to other more affluent sectors."[313] Of course, their business acumen led them to keep their old properties and use them solely for commercial purposes.

(...) When they left Patronato as a residence and not at all interested in selling the properties, many families preferred to take advantage of them as a retail location. (...)Patronato was particularly suitable for this purpose. The continuous facade allowed for an easy transformation from residential to commercial fronts, demolishing or enlarging the doorways and windows, and adapting them as showcases. The rooms and backyards, in turn, served as workshops and warehouses.[314]

This process of migration to more affluent neighborhoods is not only evidence of a higher standard of living of future generations, but is also considered a process of social integration. The descendants left the predominantly Arab neighborhoods, and settled in diverse parts of the city, sharing it with their Chilean neighbors.

As remembered by Kamel Jadue Jarufe:

Over time, the Palestinians began to spread. They began to move from Patronato, buying homes in other neighborhoods. No more business was done at home. They began to sell their homes for business, because it was much more profitable. With the sale of a store in the neighborhood, they could buy four houses. They went to Irarrázaval, Providencia, some to Ñuñoa and Kennedy Avenue.[315] There is no more trade on Perú Avenue. There are only restaurants. Others bought land in Lonquén, Buin, Paine ,[316] also in the south: Villarrica, Pucón, Osorno, La Unión, Valdivia, etc.[317]

Over the years, this tendency increased. According to the EPOA survey,[318] the current geographic distribution of the Arab population was heavily concentrated, up to 53%, in upper-middle class communes and districts (such as Lo Barnechea, Vitacura, Las Condes, and Providencia) on the east side of Santiago. In communes typically considered middle-class (La Reina and Providencia) it is 15%, while 29% is found in other sectors.

Even today there are still some remnants of Palestinian immigrants in Patronato, such as shops, restaurants, the St. George Orthodox Church, and there are even some retailers who sell hollowed potatoes and grape leaves [319] on the street. However, at the beginning of the 1980s, the area started changing and welcoming new immigrant groups, especially Koreans, who had a strong presence on the streets engaging in the same business activities as the Palestinian community.

Discrimination: A Problem for the Early Immigrants

At first, the Palestinian immigrants were not viewed favorably by the Chilean society in general. Their different appearance, customs, and mispronounced Spanish contrasted and shocked the average Chilean, inciting discrimination. That most lived in the poor sectors and their expenses were limited to the most basic needs also added insult to injury.

As explained by Ruiz and Sáiz:
> The Arabs aroused great suspicion for many reasons, among which was language, since the vast majority of these immigrants only knew Arabic or were illiterate. Furthermore, their customs were totally alien to those of the host societies.[320]

A passage quoted by Olguín and Peña that reflects the Chileans resentment on the newcomers:
> You will have noticed that the Turks... open early. They close when not a single soul passes. If no one comes, they remain motionless saving in energy and clothing. They live in large houses. How many live there? Only God knows. Have you seen them enter? They are like ants. After a few years, they open their factory and nothing changes: they wear the same clothes, their appearance is the same, their manner is the same. Only by what is in their factory one realizes that they are rich. [321]

The Arabs in general were often treated derogatorily, both in daily contact and through the local press. For example, one of the leading intellectuals of the time, Joaquín Edwards Bello, expressed concern that the immigration of "Arabs, Syrians, and Jews," was the cause of the Chileans "darker skin color" in neighborhoods such as Recoleta, San Pablo and San Diego, but in reality the mixed and indigenous traits had always been present in the local population. "The intellectual group of the early twentieth century, a paradigmatic representative of the oligarchic class, often manifested in a derogatory manner in relation to Arab immigrants, but also about all sectors that had no central European origin." [322]

Even when they began to acquire economic wealth, they still suffered discriminatory treatment. As Daher recounts, "one of the traditional clubs, once an aristocratic bastion, lost its distinction precisely due to the need to maintain a lavish location in the heart of the capital, granting admission to some very rich Turks."[323]

Paradoxically, the Palestinians were aware that they had reached an equally underdeveloped country as their homeland, and that it did not even possess a fraction of the splendor of the Arabic culture that has made notable contributions to the world in various disciplines. So, feeling discriminated against by people who they in no way considered better socio-culturally, they opted to retreat.[324]

However, the Palestinian immigrants had complete freedom to develop trade and business, study, and settle in the country. Although they suffered some social exclusion, they were not subject to any action or deliberate campaign of persecution of any kind.

Since the first immigrants of Arab origin entered the continent with Ottoman passports, they were treated as "Turks" by the host societies. Latin Americans knew little about the different nationalities in the Arab world, so they grouped Palestinians, Syrians, Lebanese, and other Middle Eastern immigrants under the same name. Undoubtedly this adjective was used primarily in a pejorative sense. Of course this nickname hit hard to those who had just arrived fleeing the Ottoman Empire.

Their descendants also received the same appellation, particularly at school, and since school is key in the process of socialization, it was difficult to integrate. According to the EPOA survey [325] (Agar, 2009), 81% of businessmen and 62% of academic respondents (most first or second generations born in Chile) admitted to being called "Turk" by their peers. However, only 36% of the students surveyed, (many from the third generation born in the country,) claimed to have received this nickname, reflecting the integration process of the descendants over time.

Integration and Roots Rescue

After more than a century of Palestinian immigration to the country, we can say that their descendants – either paternal last name, maternal, or both – are estimated at about between 150,000-200,000 people,[326] and actively participate as part of the Chilean society. Although the first

78

immigrants had no formal education, they insisted that their children should study. They wanted to have a better future and with more opportunities. Many of them benefited from quality public education offered by the State in the mid-twentieth century, with its emblematic institutions like the National Institute and the University of Chile, where many of the country's leaders have been formed.

Not only did their descendants study, but it was during school and university where the majority of the integration occurred. This is where they learned to speak the language properly and they often served as "interpreters" to their parents. They shared with their Chilean colleagues, made friends, and even married. They were seen as part of the society, not as foreigners but as Chileans.

The fruits of this process are abundant. The entrepreneurial spirit of the Palestinians and their descendants has allowed for an invaluable contribution to the Chilean economy. The new generations of Palestinians contribute with much success in various areas of society such as the exact sciences, social sciences, humanities, and the arts. In politics, the unusual number of area representatives and senators from Middle Eastern backgrounds formed in Congress in what is known as the "Palestinian caucus", or in groups composed of parliamentarians from different political parties yet united by their roots and their interest in Palestine.

In fact, it is important to highlight as a major achievement the Chilean government's recognition of the Palestinian State in January 2011.[327] The Chilean government has supported permanently and consistently the rights of the Palestinian people. It recognizes the Palestinian existence as a free, independent, and sovereign state. In that statement, it also recognizes the Palestinian community in Chile "for its valuable contribution to the social, cultural, political, and economic development over many decades and its full integration into our society."

This was reaffirmed by Kamel Jadue Jarufe:
> Eminent doctors, lawyers, teachers, politicians, and athletes that have given prestige to Chile at the international level, are of Arab descent. Just as important industrialists, bankers, and traders. (...) And in their heart they hold a heartfelt remembrance of respect and affection for the wonderful example of dignity and strength that their grandparents and distant homelands gave so they could advance. They do not forget that thanks to the sacrifices of their ancestors, they can look calmly to the future.[328]

However, the successful integration has also meant a process of assimilation of cultural elements of the Chilean society, with consequent loss of some distinctive features. The loss of the language is the most obvious indication. As shown, Marcela Zedán, director of the Center for Arab Studies at the University of Chile, says the number of people who have a command of the language in Chile is only 2,000. This is due to their being born in an Arab country. It is estimated that a similar number of offspring learned the language in their households, so their domain is oral. At the same time, there are about 5,000 people studying Arabic at various levels that exist in the country, reaching different levels of knowledge.[329]

Moreover, many immigrants changed their last names to facilitate both business and personal relationships. "With the change, the following Arab families were born: Campos, Flores, Martínez, Pinto, García, Díaz, and Tapia. They also changed their first names; Issa changed to Salvador, Hanna to Juan, Muhammad to Manuel, Jalil to Julio, among many others."[330] With this, many families lost their Arab roots forever.

These same marriages with Chileans, which had facilitated the social integration, have also contributed to the loss of values and customs of Palestinian families. In fact, couples sharing the same origin is no longer a predominant factor when it comes to marriage. According to the EPOA survey,[331] 56% of the respondents stated that it is not important for the spouses of their children to be of Arab origin, while only 13% of the students said it is important to marry a person of the same origin.

However, younger generations still conserve or seek to rediscover their roots. Hence, grape leaves and hummus [332] can still be seen on the tables in the Palestinian homes with Arabic music playing in the background. In this regard, the survey conducted at the Arabic School of students with both parents of the same origin, 75% reported practicing Arab traditions and 25% said they do so on occasion. With students with one parent of Palestinian origin, the proportion is reversed: 21% said they practice these traditions and 68% said they sometimes do.

Chileans have also experienced some elements of the Palestinian culture. There are several Arabic food restaurants that exist in both Santiago and the provinces. Arabic dance academies have also experienced a real "boom" in recent years. Their customers considerably exceed the community's population.

When defining their identity, the majority of the descendants gave two homelands, the inherited one and the one in which they were born. According to the EPOA survey,[333] 65% of the respondents recognized themselves as "Chilean/Arab", although this percentage decreases in younger descendants (20%). Among the Arabic School students surveyed, 60% said they feel "Chilean/Arab" and 38% said "Arab". They also acknowledged that they inherited many of the values of their parents and grandparents, such as responsibility, hard work, determination, independence, and perseverance.

There are several organizations established in the country that seek to keep the Palestinian culture and community spirit alive, including the Palestinian Sports Club, founded in 1920. It was the first soccer team in the world to bear the name and colors of the Palestinian flag and is currently in Chile's first division. The Palestinian Club, founded in 1947, is another organization for the community; the Centre for Arab Studies at the University of Chile, formed in 1966, holds history and Arabic courses; the Arabic School, established in 1978, educates Arab children and youth and is open to all Chilean society; the General Union of Palestinian Students (UGEP-Chile), which was created in the late-1980s by the youth seeking to support the creation of a Palestinian state. Another institution is the Palestinian Bethlehem 2000 Foundation, created in 2001, which seeks to unite the Arab community in Chile and help the Palestinian people.

In order to preserve the Orthodox worship, in the year 1978 a group of Arab youth, led by José Elías and Gabriel Salvador, decided to establish a new temple in the commune of Providencia. Thus was born the Church of the Santísima Virgen María (Blessed Virgin Mary), in what was once the Protestant temple belonging to the Union Church. The masses, unlike the Cathedral of St. George, were in Spanish. "The motto of this church was openness and integration with the Chilean community. Padre Francisco Salvador insisted that being proud of one's origins is not incompatible with being Chilean."[334]

Moreover, the Israeli occupation of Palestinian territories and the precarious conditions in which they find their people have reinforced the feeling of unity and solidarity within the Palestinian community in Chile. Furthermore, it should be noted that many of its members still maintain ties with their relatives living in the land of their ancestors.

According to the EPOA survey,[335] 90% of respondents claimed to identify with the Palestinian cause. Touzri explains, "(...) the social impact of the tragic conditions that the Palestinian people in the Middle East suffer and the appreciation of national identity have enhanced the continuity of the Arab and Palestinian communities, especially as a whole."[336]

The feeling of being part of the Palestinian and Arab community in general is high and, moreover, is a major contribution to the Chilean society. This is reflected in the study at the Arab School, in which 90% felt as part of the community and a nearly unanimous 97% said that this community has been a contribution to Chile.[337]

Final Words

In conclusion, we can see that at the beginning, the Palestinian community, and Arabs in general, were discriminated against by the Chilean society due to poor language skills, their dedication to economic activities in the lower socio-economic classes, and the overall differences in their customs. However, factors such as shared religious values, open trade relations, acquirement of financial resources, education, mixed marriages, and the settling in different sectors of the capital and the country allowed for a rapid integration into Chilean society.

In turn, this process also involved some loss of cultural elements and values. However, the new generations have remained united as a group, encouraged by the work of a number of Arab social organizations and the sense of identification with the Palestinian cause. Although the descendants consider themselves Chilean, the first, second, third, and even fourth generations born in the country somehow still identify themselves as Arabs.

Although the first settlers crossed the mountains more than a century ago, their descendants were well aware that without the work and initiative of their parents and grandparents, Chile would not be the country it is today, and so, this has generated a sense of belonging and pride. The members of the Palestinian community are known for their entrepreneurial spirit as start-up pioneers. Today, most are professionals who excel in the diverse fields of economy, politics, and social affairs. Many have lost their language and much of the traditions, but their roots remain present, reborn in every generation, making them feel part of a community with two anchors: Palestinian and Chilean.

Endnotes

1. It is worthwhile mentioning that in recent years a discussion regarding a new perspective on the Palestinians abroad has been going on also among Palestinians themselves. Rethinking the language and the terms used so far such as "Palestinian refugees", "Al Schatat" and others while considering applying concepts such as Diaspora in referring to the Palestinians abroad. Nevertheless, some studies that call for the use of the concept Diaspora underline at the same time that this concept does not apply fully to the Descendents of Palestinians in Latin America, since they are an assimilated population within their new countries. See Sari Hanafi, "Rethinking the Palestinians Abroad as a Diaspora: The relationship between the Diaspora and the Palestinian Territories:" in: Andreh Levi, Alex Weingrod, *Homelands and Diasporas: Holy Lands and Other Places*, Stanford University Press 2005, pp. 97-122.

2   p. 43.

3   p. 79.

4   p. 54.

5   To name but few, Jorge Safady, *Antologia Arabe do Brasil*, Jamil Safady, *A cultura Arabe no Brasil, Libano e Síria*, Jeffrey Lesser and Ignacio Klich, *Arab and Jewish Immigrants in Latin America: Images and Realities* Roberto Marin-Guzman, Zidane Zeraoui, *Arab Immigration in Mexico in the Nineteenth and Twentieth Centuries: Assimilation and Arab Heritage*, Nancie L. González *One Hundred Years of Palestinian Migration to Honduras*, Leyla Bartet, Farid Kahhat, *La huella árabe en el Perú*.

6   In May 2008, the UCLA International Institute held a Symposium on Middle Eastern Communities in Latin America, which was aimed at initiating a broader research project on the theme. In May 2011 the Institute for Migration Studies, Department of Social Sciences, Lebanese American University, Beirut, Lebanon and the Department of Geography, Johannes Gutenberg-Universität, Mainz, Germany organized an International Conference on the theme "Palestinian, Lebanese and Syrian communities in the world: Theoretical frameworks and empirical studies."

7   Nancie L. Gonzalez, Carolyn S. McCommon. 1989.

8   Olivier Prud'homme, 2006.

9   Rosa Araya Suazo, 1986.

10 Maria Narbona, *Islam and Muslims in Latin America: An Overview*, Raymond Delval, *Les musulmans en Amérique Latine et aux Caraibes*, Pedro Brieger , Enrique Herszkowich, *The Muslim Community of Argentina*.

11 Judith Laikin Elkin, Gilbert W. Merkx (eds.), *The Jewish Presence in Latin America*, David Sheinin, Lois Baer Barr (eds.), *The Jewish Diaspora in Latin America: New Studies on History and Literature*, Victor A Mirelman, *Jewish Buenos Aires 1890-1930. In Search of an Identity*, Robert M. Levine, *Tropical Diaspora, The Jewish Experience in Cuba*.

12 For example: Waltraut Kokot, Khachig Tölölyan, Carolin Alfonso (ed.), *Diaspora, Identity and Religion. New Directions in Theory and Research*, 2004, *Peter Beyer, B. Clarke Peter, The World's Religions: Continuities and Transformations*.

13 Karpat, 2002, p.103.

14 Orthodox Archbishop of Chile, http://www.chileortodoxo.cl/arqui.html

15 p. 67.

16 p. 30.

17 Gonzalez, 1992, Musalem Rahal, 1997

18 Al Qass Collings, Odeh Kassis, Raheb, 2008, p. 6.

19 Farah, 2003, p. 147.

20 Marín-Guzmán, 2000, pp. 95-109.

21 Adnan Musallam, *A Nation of Immigrants: The Arab Immigrant Experience in America*, Curriculum Development Center (Outreach Program), Center for Near Eastern and North African Studies, The University of Michigan, Ann Arbor, Michigan, 1981, p.6.

22 Kemal H. Karpat, "The Ottoman Emigration to America, 1860-1914", *International Journal of Middle East Studies*, Vol. 17, 2 (May 1985), p. 85

23 Ibid.

24 Adnan Musallam, p. 6

25 Ahmad Tarabin, "Aspects of Syrian Arab Emigration to the United States,": in *Damascus University Journal*, Vol.2, June 1985, p.19. (in Arabic); and Adnan Musallam, *A Nation of Immigrants*, p. 13.

26 Kemal H. Karpat, p.179.

27 Charles Issawi, *An Economic History of the Middle East and North Africa*, New York, 1982, p.86

28 For details see the classical works on the subject: George Antonius, *The Arab Awakening: The Story of the Arab National Movement*, Philadelphia, New York, Toronto: J.B. Lippincott, 1939; and Albert Hourani, *A History of the Arab Peoples*, New York: Warner Books, 1991. For the incomplete list of families in Bethlehem's Seven Traditional Clans/Quarters in the Early 20th century: 'Anatreh, Farahiyye, Fawaghreh, Kawawseh, Najajreh, Tarajmah, and Hreizat, compiled by Adnan Ayyub Musallam. See Web-site admusallam.bethlehem.edu.

29 Kemal H. Karpat, pp. 177, 186

30 Philip Hitti, *History of Syria, Lebanon and Palestine*, Vol.2, Translated by Kamal al-Yazigi, Beirut 1959, p.357 (in Arabic).

31 Mike George Salman, "Emigration and its effect on the extinction of Bethlehem families,": in *Al-Liqa'* (in Arabic), 4th Year, Vol. l, 1989, p.55.

32 Al-Badawi al-Mulatham, *Arabic Speakers in South America* (in Arabic), part one, Beirut 1956, p.101,107.

33 Ayyub Musalam "Pages from the Book: Bethlehem in the Depth of History and as Described by Travellers and Historians,": in *Bait Lahm* (The Antonian Society Bulletin) (in Arabic), Vol.2, 1987, p.15

34 Clair Price, "Bethlehem under the British,": in *The Living Age*, vol. 305, no. 3962, June 20, 1920, p. 630

35 Al-Badawi al-Mulatham, p.107.

36 May Kaileh, "Palestinian Christians in Chile," paper prepared by the Palestinian Ambassador in Chile, *for the 9th International Conference of the Holy Land Christian Ecumenical Foundation, Washington, D.C. USA, 26 – 29 October 2007* (see www.hcef.org/index, pp. 1 – 8)

37 Adnan Musallam, pp. 10-11

38 *Palestine Royal Commission Report*. CMD 5479. London, H.M.S.O. 1937, p.330.

39 Mike Salman, pp.56-59; and Giries Elali, *Bethlehem, The Immortal town*, Bethlehem, 1991, pp. 72-8 1

40 Walid Rabi', "Emigration and Alienation in Palestinian Society, a Folkloric Social Study,": in *Society and Heritage*, Number 3, Vol.1, October 1974, p.58 (in Arabic).

41 *Palestine Royal Commission Report, CMD* 5479, p.329.

42 Lauren E. Banko, "The Legislative Creation of Palestinian Citizenship: Discourse in the Early Mandate Period,": in *International Journal for Arab Studies,* Vol. 2, No. 2, July 2011, p. 2.

43 Ibid., p. 5.

44 Ibid., p. 6.

45 Ibid.,

46 Ibid., p. 21

47 Ibid.,

48 *A collection of Documents Relating to the Political, Economic, and Educational History of Palestine During the British Mandate, 1909 – 1939*, collected, prepared and introduced by Hammad Hussein, Jenin, the West Bank, PNA, Publications of the Palestinian Center for Culture and Mass Media, 2003, pp. 168 – 202 (in Arabic).

49 *Palestine Royal Commission Report*, CMD 5479, p. 331

50 Ibid, pp.330-331.

51 Preparatory Committee for the Defense of the Rights of Arab Emigrants to Palestinian Citizenship, *An Appeal to the Noble British People,* Jerusalem, 1 February 1928, pp. 8 – 9 (in Arabic).

52 Ibid, p. 9.

53 Ibid. p. 16.

54 Ibid. p. 37

55 Ibid. pp. 20 - 31

56 Ibid. p. 29.

57 Ibid. pp. 19 – 20, 32 0 34.

58 Ibid. pp. 32 – 34.

59 al-Badawi al-Mulattam, pp. 181-219.

60 al-Quds (East Jerusalem daily), Monthly Supplement, Friday 6 April, 1990, p.3. (in Arabic)

61 Sa'd al-Din Tawfiq, The Story of the Cinema in Egypt, Al-Qahira: al-Hilal Publishing Press, 1969, pp. 18-20, (in Arabic); and on Badr and Ibrahim Lama, their life and works in the cinema, see Adnan Musallam, Folded Pages from Local Palestinian History: Developments in Politicsa, Society, Press and Thought in Bethlehem in the British Era, 1917-1948, Bethlehem, 2002 (in both English and Arabic), pp. 57-66 (in Arabic).

62 For the Palestinian immigrants in Mexico, for example see: Doris Musalem, «La migración palestina en México. 1893-1949»: in María Elena Ota Mishima, editor, Destino México, El Colegio de México, Mexico, 1997, passim. See also: Theresa Alfaro-Velcamp, So Far from Allah, so Close to Mexico. Middle Eastern Immigrants in Modern Mexico, University of Texas Press, Austin, Texas, 2007, passim. Roberto Marín-Guzmán, "Los inmigrantes árabes en México en los siglos XIX Y XX. Un estudio de historia social," in Raymundo Kabchi, El Mundo Árabe y América Latina, Ediciones UNESCO y Libertarias, Madrid, 1997, pp. 123-154. Zidane Zéraoui, "Los árabes en México: entre la integración y el arabismo," in Revista Estudios, Numbers 12-13, 1995-1996, pp. 13-39. Roberto Marín-Guzmán and Zidane Zéraoui, Arab immigration in Mexico in the Nineteenth and Twentieth centuries. Assimilation and Arab heritage, Augustin Press and Instituto Tecnológico de Monterrey, Austin, Texas and Monterrey, Mexico, 2003, passim. Roberto Marín-Guzmán, "Al-Muhajirun al-'Arab fi al-Maksik Khilal al-Qarnayn al-Tasi' 'Ashar wa al-'Ashryin", in 'Abd al-Wahid Akmir, editor, Al-Watan al-'Arabi wa Amirika al-Latiniyya, Markaz Dirasat al-Wahda al-'Arabiyya, Beirut, 2005, pp.93-116.

63 Palestinian immigrants also arrived to Panama. However, the study of the Palestinian immigrants to this country goes beyond the scope of this essay.

64 In the statistical data gathered by the various foreign travelers in Central America, contained in this table, Costa Rica does not appear. However, it is necessary to point out that for those years, when travelers passed by the isthmus, there were already two last names of Palestinian origin in Costa Rica: the last name of the Bakit (Bakhit) family and the Hasbun family. These two last names have been included in this table hoping to complete the statistical data missing in the travelers' reports.

65 In that time it was known that some Arabs had started a few new industries, since the beginning of the Twentieth century. The first case was a cigarette factory that was established by an Arab in San Pedro Sula in 1914. From existing sources it is impossible to determine if this Arab was of Palestinian origin or if he was Syrian or Lebanese. It was also known at that time that it was a group of Arabs, probably of Palestinian origin and Christian faith, who first started selling ground coffee in the streets of San Pedro Sula. For more information see: Nancie L. González, Dollar, Dove and Eagle. One Hundred Years of Palestinian Migration to Honduras, The University of Michigan Press, Ann Arbor, 1992, p. 93. Roberto Marín-Guzmán, "El aporte económico y cultural de la inmigración árabe en Centro América en los siglos XIX y XX," in Raymundo Kabchi, El Mundo Árabe y América Latina, Ediciones UNESCO y Libertarias, Madrid, 1997, pp. 155-198. Marín-Guzmán, "Los inmigrantes árabes en México," passim. Zéraoui, "Los árabes en México," passim. For more details see also: Roberto Marín-Guzmán, A Century of Palestinian Immigration into Central America. A Study of Their Economic and Cultural Contributions, Editorial de la Universidad de Costa Rica, San José, Costa Rica, 2000, passim. Roberto Marín-Guzmán, "Al-Musahama al-Iqtisadiyya wa al-Thaqafiyya li'l-Muhajirin al-'Arab fi Amirika al-Wusta Khilal al-Qarnayn al-Tasi' 'Ashar wa al-'Ashryin", in 'Abd al-Wahid Akmir editor, Al-Watan al-'Arabi wa Amirika al-Latiniyya, Markaz Dirasat al-Wahda al-'Arabiyya, Beirut, 2005, pp. 117-150.

66 For more information see: The Statistical Abstract of Palestine 1944-1945, passim. For more information see also: Marín-Guzmán, "Al-Musahama al-Iqtisadiyya wa al-Thaqafiyya li'l-Muhajirin al-'Arab fi Amirika al-Wusta Khilal al-Qarnayn al-Tasi' 'Ashar wa al-'Ashryin", pp. 117-150. Marín-Guzmán, A Century of Palestinian Immigration into Central America. A Study of Their Economic and Cultural Contributions, passim, especially pp.26-41.

67 For more information see: William K. Crowley, «The Levantine Arabs: Diaspora in the New World,» in *Proceedings of the Association of American Geographers*, Number 6, 1974, pp. 137-142.

68 For more information see: Marcos Martínez, «Los hondureños de origen árabe», in *Aljama. Revista Arabo-Centroamericana*, Vol. I, Number 3, September-December, 1990, pp. 15-16, especially p. 16. For more information see also: Marín-Guzmán, "Al-Musahama al-Iqtisadiyya wa al-Thaqafiyya li'l-Muhajirin al-'Arab fi Amirika al-Wusta Khilal al-Qarnayn al-Tasi' 'Ashar wa al-'Ashryin", pp. 117-150. Marín-Guzmán, *A Century of Palestinian Immigration into Central America. A Study of Their Economic and Cultural Contributions*, passim, especially pp.26-41.

69 For more details see: Martínez, «Los hondureños de origen árabe,» p. 16. For more information see also: Marín-Guzmán, "Al-Musahama al-Iqtisadiyya wa al-Thaqafiyya li'l-Muhajirin al-'Arab fi Amirika al-Wusta Khilal al-Qarnayn al-Tasi' 'Ashar wa al-'Ashryin", pp. 117-150. Marín-Guzmán, *A Century of Palestinian Immigration into Central America. A Study of Their Economic and Cultural Contributions*, passim, especially pp.26-41.

70 See: González, *Dollar*, passim, especially pp. 23 ff. See also: Kemal H. Karpat, "The Ottoman Emigration to America, 1860-1914," in *International Journal of Middle East Studies*, Vol. XVII, 1985, pp. 175-209, especially p.180 and pp.188-189. Concerning the percentages of Palestinian Muslims see: Karpat, "Ottoman Emigration," passim, especially p.180. See also: Marín-Guzmán, "El aporte económico y cultural," passim. Marín-Guzmán, "Los inmigrantes árabes en México," passim. Zéraoui, "Los árabes en México," passim.

71 Scholars have pointed out numerous reasons for the emigration of the Palestinians, most of them Christians. One of the most convincing motives seems to have been the fact that the Ottoman authorities established, in 1909, military drafting also mandatory for Christians. This military drafting really meant that the Christian populations actually had to go to the war. Because of this, many of them emigrated in order to avoid this military experience. For more details see: Philip Hitti, *Arabs. A Short History*, Gateways Editions, London, 1965, p. 242. It has also been pointed out that many Palestinians emigrated without a clear destination. For example, it is possible to mention the case of a Levantine who, after being in Australia for two years, realized that he was not in New York. According to informants in Honduras and in interviews with the eldest ones, the great majority of the Palestinian immigrants in Honduras had planned their destination in advance. The motives were either to join relatives in Honduras or to start new businesses, following the example of so many in this host country. Most of them hoped to obtain great profits from their commercial activities. For more details see: R.B. Houghton, *Central Americans from the Arab World*, U.S. Department of State, Washington D.C., 1969-1970 (unpublished), quoted by González, *Dollar*, p. 64. Marín-Guzmán, "El aporte económico y cultural," passim. Marín-Guzmán, "Los inmigrantes árabes en México", passim. Zéraoui, "Los árabes en México," passim. For more information see also: Marín-Guzmán, "Al-Musahama al-Iqtisadiyya wa al-Thaqafiyya li'l-Muhajirin al-'Arab fi Amirika al-Wusta Khilal al-Qarnayn al-Tasi' 'Ashar wa al-'Ashryin", pp. 117-150. Marín-Guzmán, *A Century of Palestinian Immigration into Central America. A Study of Their Economic and Cultural Contributions*, passim, especially pp.26-41.

72 For more details see: Nellie Ammar, «They came from the Middle East,» in *Jamaica Journal*, Vol. IV, Number 1, 1970, pp. 2-6, see especially p. 4. See also: González, *Dollar*, p. 69. Marín-Guzmán, "El aporte económico y cultural", passim. For more information see also: Marín-Guzmán, "Al-Musahama al-Iqtisadiyya wa al-Thaqafiyya li'l-Muhajirin al-'Arab fi Amirika al-Wusta Khilal al-Qarnayn al-Tasi' 'Ashar wa al-'Ashryin", pp. 117-150. Marín-Guzmán, *A Century of Palestinian Immigration into Central America. A Study of Their Economic and Cultural Contributions*, passim, especially pp.26-41.

73 Since the beginning of the economic progress of the northern coast of Honduras, this area became a banana enclave. For this reason the northern coast was more related and in better communications with other countries, rather than with the interior regions of Honduras. At the beginning of the Twentieth century a trip from La Ceiba to New Orleans took three days, and at the same time from La Ceiba to Tegucigalpa the trip could have taken one week or longer if it was on the back of a mule. For more information about all these issues see: Mario Posas, "La Plantación Bananera en Centro América (1870-1929)," in Víctor Hugo Acuña, *Historia General de Centro América*, Vol. IV "Las Repúblicas Bananeras", FLACSO, San José, 1994, pp.111-165, especially pp. 111-112.

74 For more information see: Karl T. Sapper, *Mexico, Land, Volk und Wirtschaft*, L.W. Seidel, Vienna, 1928, pp. 429-430, quoted by González, *Dollar*, pp. 70-71. See also: Marín-Guzmán, "El aporte económico y cultural," passim.

For more information see also: Marín-Guzmán, "Al-Musahama al-Iqtisadiyya wa al-Thaqafiyya li'l-Muhajirin al-'Arab fi Amirika al-Wusta Khilal al-Qarnayn al-Tasi' 'Ashar wa al-'Ashryin", pp. 117-150. Marín-Guzmán, *A Century of Palestinian Immigration into Central America. A Study of Their Economic and Cultural Contributions*, passim, especially pp.26-41.

75   For more details see: González, *Dollar*, passim, especially pp.93-95. Ramiro Luque, "Memorias de un sanpedrano," (unpublished), quoted by González, *Dollar*, p.93. Marín-Guzmán, "El aporte económico y cultural," passim. For more information see also: Interview with doctor Norma Handal, San José, Costa Rica, March 20, 1995. Doctor Handal is a Honduran psychiatrist, a Palestinian immigrant of Christian origin. She resides now in Costa Rica. For more information see also: Marín-Guzmán, "Al-Musahama al-Iqtisadiyya wa al-Thaqafiyya li'l-Muhajirin al-'Arab fi Amirika al-Wusta Khilal al-Qarnayn al-Tasi' 'Ashar wa al-'Ashryin", pp. 117-150. Marín-Guzmán, *A Century of Palestinian Immigration into Central America. A Study of Their Economic and Cultural Contributions*, passim, especially pp.26-41.

76   González, *Dollar*, p.95. See also: Interview with doctor Norma Handal, San José, Costa Rica, March 20, 1995. In Costa Rica there were some Palestinian immigrants who practiced a modern form of itinerant commerce in the 1990s and also early at the beginning of the new millennium. That was the case of 'Abd al-Karim Tahir, although he is a Muslim. See also: Interview with 'Abd al-Karim Tahir, San José, Costa Rica, March 25, 1995, and also: Interview with 'Abd al-Karim Tahir, San José, Costa Rica, April 1, 1995. For more information see: Marín-Guzmán, "El aporte económico y cultural," passim. See also: Marín-Guzmán, "Al-Musahama al-Iqtisadiyya wa al-Thaqafiyya li'l-Muhajirin al-'Arab fi Amirika al-Wusta Khilal al-Qarnayn al-Tasi' 'Ashar wa al-'Ashryin", pp. 117-150. Marín-Guzmán, *A Century of Palestinian Immigration into Central America. A Study of Their Economic and Cultural Contributions*, passim, especially pp.26-41.

77   See: González, *Dollar*, p. 106. See also: Marín-Guzmán, "El aporte económico y cultural," passim. For more information see also: Marín-Guzmán, "Al-Musahama al-Iqtisadiyya wa al-Thaqafiyya li'l-Muhajirin al-'Arab fi Amirika al-Wusta Khilal al-Qarnayn al-Tasi' 'Ashar wa al-'Ashryin", pp. 117-150. Marín-Guzmán, *A Century of Palestinian Immigration into Central America. A Study of Their Economic and Cultural Contributions*, passim, especially pp.26-41.

78   For more information see: Marín-Guzmán, «El aporte económico y cultural,» passim. See also: González, *Dollar*, p. 106. For more information see also: Marín-Guzmán, "Al-Musahama al-Iqtisadiyya wa al-Thaqafiyya li'l-Muhajirin al-'Arab fi Amirika al-Wusta Khilal al-Qarnayn al-Tasi' 'Ashar wa al-'Ashryin", pp. 117-150. Marín-Guzmán, *A Century of Palestinian Immigration into Central America. A Study of Their Economic and Cultural Contributions*, passim, especially pp.26-41.

79   See: Marín-Guzmán, «El aporte económico y cultural,» passim. See also: González, *Dollar*, p. 103. Interview with doctor Norma Handal, San José, Costa Rica, March 20, 1995. For more information see also: Marín-Guzmán, "Al-Musahama al-Iqtisadiyya wa al-Thaqafiyya li'l-Muhajirin al-'Arab fi Amirika al-Wusta Khilal al-Qarnayn al-Tasi' 'Ashar wa al-'Ashryin", pp.117-150. Marín-Guzmán, *A Century of Palestinian Immigration into Central America. A Study of Their Economic and Cultural Contributions*, passim, especially pp.26-41.

80   For more information concerning the practice of endogamy in the early periods of Palestinian immigration in Honduras, see: González, *Dollar*, pp. 116-120. For the Palestinian and other Arab immigrants in the other countries of Central America, see: Marín-Guzmán, "El aporte económico y cultural," passim.

81   See: Marín-Guzmán, «El aporte económico y cultural,» passim. See also: González, *Dollar*, p. 103. For more information see also: Marín-Guzmán, "Al-Musahama al-Iqtisadiyya wa al-Thaqafiyya li'l-Muhajirin al-'Arab fi Amirika al-Wusta Khilal al-Qarnayn al-Tasi' 'Ashar wa al-'Ashryin", pp. 117-150. Marín-Guzmán, *A Century of Palestinian Immigration into Central America. A Study of Their Economic and Cultural Contributions*, passim, especially pp.26-41.

82   Vanessa Barahona, "Jacobo Kattan, textilero de la moda", in *Summa*, Number 172, 2008, pp.27-36, especially p.27. See also: Roberto Marín-Guzmán, "Los árabes en Centroamérica", in Abdeluahed Akmir, *Los Árabes en América Latina. Historia de una emigración*, Casa Árabe, Siglo XXI, Madrid, 2009, pp.429-501, especially p.456.

83   Barahona, "Jacobo Kattan, textilero de la moda", pp.27-36. For more information see also: Marín-Guzmán, "Los árabes en Centroamérica", p.456.

84 For more information see: Barahona, "Jacobo Kattan, textilero de la moda", pp.27-36. See also: Marín-Guzmán, "Los árabes en Centroamérica, p.456.

85 For more details see: Marín-Guzmán, «El aporte económico y cultural,» passim. See also: González, *Dollar*, p. 77. Interview with doctor Norma Handal, San José, Costa Rica, March 20, 1995. Interview with Dr. 'Abd al-Fattah Sa'sa', San José, Costa Rica, October 10, 2007. Interview with Dr. 'Abd al-Fattah Sa'sa', San José, Costa Rica, June 20, 2008.

86 For more information see: González, *Dollar*, *passim*. Interview with doctor Norma Handal, San José, Costa Rica, March 20, 1995.

87 Martínez, «Los hondureños de origen árabe», p.16. For more information see also: Marín-Guzmán, «El aporte económico y cultural», passim. See also: Marín-Guzmán, "Al-Musahama al-Iqtisadiyya wa al-Thaqafiyya li'l-Muhajirin al-'Arab fi Amirika al-Wusta Khilal al-Qarnayn al-Tasi' 'Ashar wa al-'Ashryin", pp. 117-150. Marín-Guzmán, *A Century of Palestinian Immigration into Central America. A Study of Their Economic and Cultural Contributions*, passim, especially pp.26-41.

88 See: González, *Dollar*, p. 139. See also: Marín-Guzmán, "El aporte económico y cultural," passim.

89 González, *Dollar*, p. 139. Marín-Guzmán, "El aporte económico y cultural,"passim.

90 For more information concerning the *Intifada* movement in the Occupied Territories see: Raja Shehadeh, *Occupier's Law. Israel and the West Bank*, Institute for Palestine Studies, Washington, D.C., 1988, pp. 209-224. Zakariya Muhammad, "AI-Intifada wa al-Islah al-Tanzimi fi Munazamat al- Tahrir al-Filastiniyya", in *AI-Fikr al-Dimuqrati*, Number 5, 1989, p. 30. For a different version see also: Ze'ev Schiff and Ehud Ya'ari, *Intifada. The Palestinian Uprising. Israel's Third Front*, Simon and Schuster, New York, 1989, passim. For more information concerning the Fundamentalist movement in Palestine during the Intifada, see: Ziad Abu-Amr, *Islamic Fundamentalism in the West Bank and Gaza. Muslim Brotherhood and Islamic Jihad*, Indiana University Press, Bloomington, 1994, passim. Salih Wardani, *AI-Haraka al- Islamiyya wa al-Qadiyya al-Filastiniyya*, Al-Dar al-Sharqiyya, Cairo, 1990, passim. Ibrahim Sarbal, *Harakat ai-Jihad al-Islami wa al-Intifada*, 'Amman, 1990, passim. Fathi 'Abd al-'Aziz al-Shaqaqi, *AI-Khumayni: al-Hall al-Islami wa al-Badil*, Al-Mukhtar al-Islami, Cairo, 1979, passim. Jean-François Legrain, "A Defining Moment: Palestinian Islamic Fundamentalism", in James Piscatori, *Islamic Fundamentalism and the Gulf Crisis*, American Academy of Arts and Sciences, Chicago, 1991, pp. 70-87. Roberto Marín-Guzmán, "El Fundamentalismo Islámico en Palestina: Doctrina y Praxis Política", in *Panorama de un mundo cambiante*, Universidad de Costa Rica, San José, Costa Rica, 1995, pp. 227-239. See also: Roberto Marín-Guzmán, "La alternativa religiosa frente al secularismo: origen, desarrollo y aspiraciones del fundamentalismo islámico en Palestina", in *Revista de Humanidades*, Number 3, 1997, pp. 213-240.

91 González, *Dollar*, pp. 139-141.

92 For more details about the political participation of Palestinian descendants in Honduras see: Martínez, «Los hondureños de origen árabe,» pp.15-16. See also: David Adams, «Los «Turcos» de Honduras,» in *Aljama. Revista Arabo-Centroamericana*, Vol. I, Number 3, September-December, 1990, pp.12-14. Marín-Guzmán, "El aporte económico y cultural," passim. For more information see also: Marín-Guzmán, "Al-Musahama al-Iqtisadiyya wa al-Thaqafiyya li'l-Muhajirin al-'Arab fi Amirika al-Wusta Khilal al-Qarnayn al-Tasi' 'Ashar wa al-'Ashryin", pp. 117-150. Marín-Guzmán, *A Century of Palestinian Immigration into Central America. A Study of Their Economic and Cultural Contributions*, passim, especially pp.26-41. See also the excellent and detailed analysis by Darío A. Euraque, "Los árabes en Honduras: entre la inmigración, la acumulación y la política", in *Contribuciones Árabes a las Identidades Iberoamericanas*, Casa Árabe, Madrid, 2009, pp.233-284.

93 For more details see: Martínez, «Los hondureños de origen árabe,» p. 16. Marín-Guzmán, «El aporte económico y cultural,» *passim*. Marín-Guzmán, "Los árabes en Centroamérica", p.458.

94 For more information see: Marín-Guzmán, «El aporte económico y cultural,» passim. González, *Dollar*, passim, especially p. 142. Martínez, "Los hondureños de origen árabe," p. 16. Adams, "Los "Turcos" de Honduras," p. 14. Interview with doctor Norma Handal, San José, Costa Rica, March 20, 1995.

95 Interview with Nijmeh (Estrella) Mu'ammar, San José, Costa Rica, March 11, 1995. Nijmeh (Estrella) Mu'ammar is a Palestinian immigrant in El Salvador, where she lived for many years. She resides now in San José, Costa Rica. Mrs. Mu'ammar pointed out that her parents and her uncles, as well as many other Palestinian immigrants arrived

in El Salvador between 1910 and 1924. Many of them had in mind to reach Chile, but, according to the oral history, due to the fact that the ship harbored in El Salvador, they decided to disembark and to visit the place. Because the ship left the port without warning, they were left in El Salvador and far away from their final destination. They decided to stay and to start their commercial activities. For more information see also: Marín-Guzmán, "El aporte económico y cultural," passim. Interview with doctor Norma Handal, San José, Costa Rica, March 20, 1995.

96 Interview with Nijmeh (Estrella) Mu'ammar, San José, Costa Rica, March 11, 1995. Interview with doctor Norma Handal, San José, Costa Rica, March 20, 1995. Interview with Dr. 'Abd al-Fattah Sa'sa', San José, Costa Rica, October 10, 2007. Interview with Dr. 'Abd al-Fattah Sa'sa', San José, Costa Rica, June 20, 2008.

97 Interview with Nijmeh (Estrella) Mu'ammar, San José, Costa Rica, March 11, 1995. For more information see also: Marín-Guzmán, «El aporte económico y cultural,» passim. Marín-Guzmán, "Al-Musahama al-Iqtisadiyya wa al-Thaqafiyya li'l-Muhajirin al-'Arab fi Amirika al-Wusta Khilal al-Qarnayn al-Tasi' 'Ashar wa al-'Ashryin", pp. 117-150. Marín-Guzmán, *A Century of Palestinian Immigration into Central America. A Study of Their Economic and Cultural Contributions*, passim, especially pp.42-49.

98 Interview with Nijmeh (Estrella) Mu'ammar, San José, Costa Rica, March 11, 1995. Interview with Dr. 'Abd al-Fattah Sa'sa', San José, Costa Rica, October 10, 2007. Interview with Dr. 'Abd al-Fattah Sa'sa', San José, Costa Rica, June 20, 2008. For more information see also: Marín-Guzmán, "El aporte económico y cultural," passim.

99 Interview with Nijmeh (Estrella) Mu'ammar, San José, Costa Rica, March 11, 1995. For more information see also: Marín-Guzmán, «El aporte económico y cultural,» passim. Mrs. Mu'ammar in her interview affirmed that 'Isa Miguel is the owner of 40 per cent of the *Banco de La Vivienda*. However, I haven't been able to corroborate this information.

100 Interview with Nijmeh (Estrella) Mu'ammar, San José, Costa Rica, March 11, 1995. For more information see also: Marín-Guzmán, «El aporte económico y cultural,» passim. Interview with doctor Norma Handal, San José, Costa Rica, March 20, 1995. Interview with Dr. 'Abd al-Fattah Sa'sa', San José, Costa Rica, October 10, 2007. Interview with Dr. 'Abd al-Fattah Sa'sa', San José, Costa Rica, June 20, 2008. Marín-Guzmán, "Al-Musahama al-Iqtisadiyya wa al-Thaqafiyya li'l-Muhajirin al-'Arab fi Amirika al-Wusta Khilal al-Qarnayn al-Tasi' 'Ashar wa al-'Ashryin", pp. 117-150. Marín-Guzmán, *A Century of Palestinian Immigration into Central America. A Study of Their Economic and Cultural Contributions*, passim, especially pp.42-49.

101 Letter of José Alberto Brenes León, Ambassador of Costa Rica in El Salvador, February 14, 1996.

102 Marín-Guzmán, "Los árabes en Centroamérica", pp.460-461.

103 Letter of José Alberto Brenes León, Ambassador of Costa Rica in El Salvador, February 14, 1996.

104 Marín-Guzmán, "Los árabes en Centroamérica", p.461. For more information see also: Marín-Guzmán, "Al-Musahama al-Iqtisadiyya wa al-Thaqafiyya li'l-Muhajirin al-'Arab fi Amirika al-Wusta Khilal al-Qarnayn al-Tasi' 'Ashar wa al-'Ashryin", pp. 117-150. Marín-Guzmán, *A Century of Palestinian Immigration into Central America. A Study of Their Economic and Cultural Contributions*, passim, especially pp.42-49.

105 Letter of José Alberto Brenes León, Ambassador of Costa Rica in El Salvador, February 14, 1996. For more information see also: Marín-Guzmán, "Al-Musahama al-Iqtisadiyya wa al-Thaqafiyya li'l-Muhajirin al-'Arab fi Amirika al-Wusta Khilal al-Qarnayn al-Tasi' 'Ashar wa al-'Ashryin", pp. 117-150. Marín-Guzmán, *A Century of Palestinian Immigration into Central America. A Study of Their Economic and Cultural Contributions*, passim, especially pp.42-49.

106 For more details about this civil war see: Gaddis Smith, *The Last Years of the Monroe Doctrine, 1945-1993*, Hill and Wang, New York, 1994, pp. 188-193. For the American involvement in this crisis and the American military training of the Salvadoran army to stop the guerilla warfare see: Mark Danner, "The Truth of El Mozote", in *The New Yorker*, December 6, 1993, pp.50-133. See also: George P. Shultz, *Turmoil and Triumph: My Years as Secretary of State*, Scribner's Sons, New York, 1993, pp. 290-291, where he clearly explained the problems in El Salvador, as well as the troubles the American government encountered to convince Congress that major reforms were taking place and that the problems were being solved in El Salvador. He wrote: " A major problem in our assistance to El Salvador was "certification," which could stop us dead in our tracks at any time. "Certification" was Congress's way of saying it would curtail the funds needed in Central America unless we could demonstrate that notorious problems in the countries we supported were being solved -particularly the implementation of land

reform in El Salvador, the elimination of the "death squads," and progress in bringing to justice those in El Salvador who had murdered American nuns and representatives of the AFL-CIO. What this amounted to was congressional micromanagement of the U.S. economic and security assistance program..." See also the Central American press, for example: *La Nación* (San José, Costa Rica), January 7, 1990, January 8, 1990, January 9, 1990, January 10, 1990, for a detailed account of the political problems and the civil war in El Salvador.

107 For more information about Shafik Handal's participation in the Salvadoran guerrilla and in the peace process, see: *La Nación*, (San José, Costa Rica), June 20, 1990; June 21, 1990, June 22, 1990. *La Nación*, July 21, 1990; July 23, 1990. *El Diario Extra*, (San José, Costa Rica), July 24, 1990; July 25, 1990. *La Nación*, July 26, 1990. *El Diario Extra*, July 27, 1990. *La Nación*, July 27, 1990; August 26, 1990; September 1, 1990. *La Gaceta* (San José, Costa Rica), January 29, 1992. *La Nación*, October 29, 1992; December 17, 1992. *La República* (San José, Costa Rica), May 21, 1993. For more information see also: Marín-Guzmán, "Al-Musahama al-Iqtisadiyya wa al-Thaqafiyya li'l-Muhajirin al-'Arab fi Amirika al-Wusta Khilal al-Qarnayn al-Tasi' 'Ashar wa al-'Ashryin", pp. 117-150. Marín-Guzmán, *A Century of Palestinian Immigration into Central America. A Study of Their Economic and Cultural Contributions*, passim, especially pp.42-49.

108 For more information see: Víctor Hugo Murillo, «El Salvador: el poder es el problema», in *La Nación*, August 26, 1990, p. 4 C. This is an interesting interview with Shafik Handal, the guerrilla leader, and one of the top negotiators with the Salvadoran government. For more information see also: Marín-Guzmán, "Al-Musahama al-Iqtisadiyya wa al-Thaqafiyya li'l-Muhajirin al-'Arab fi Amirika al-Wusta Khilal al-Qarnayn al-Tasi' 'Ashar wa al-'Ashryin", pp. 117-150. Marín-Guzmán, *A Century of Palestinian Immigration into Central America. A Study of Their Economic and Cultural Contributions*, passim, especially pp.42-49.

109 Shafik Handal asserted that the main issue to negotiate was the change and transformation of the Salvadoran armed forces. He said: "La desmilitarización y la reducción del Ejército será el tema principal. Es el nudo gordiano para resolver la paz en nuestro país", as this is reported in *La Nación* (San José, Costa Rica), June 20, 1990.

110 Some Costa Rican journalists in their editorials pointed out that the guerrilla groups wanted to force the government to reduce the armed forces, so that the government would be weakened. Among many examples, see: *La Nación*, October 29, 1992. The author of the editorial wrote: "Shafick Handal, uno de los cinco máximos líderes de la guer-rilla, ha hecho patente, en cada fase del proceso, una permanente desconfianza acerca de la depuración en las filas militares y policiales, y la consiguiente reducción del equipo castrense. Como ha trascendido, Handal y el ala dura de la jerarquía del Frente lo que virtualmente exigen es que el Gobierno se quede indefenso, y ello para Cristiani es inaceptable, sobre todo por el ritmo de lentitud que lleva la desmovilización de los insurgentes."

111 In 1990, Rafael Angel Calderón, the Costa Rican President, offered to become a mediator in the negotiations. For this he followed the steps of Dr. Oscar Arias Sánchez, former President of Costa Rica, who was the first one to con-vince the Salvadoran government and the guerrilla groups to negotiate, and look for the mechanisms for peace in the country. President Calderón received Shafik Handal on July 26, 1992 in San José, Costa Rica. See: *La Nación*, July 27, 1992. See also: *Diario Extra* (San José, Costa Rica), July 27, 1990. This modest newspaper reported these issues with the following lines: "La firma del acuerdo de los derechos humanos logrado por el Frente Farabundo Martí para la Liberación Nacional y el Gobierno del presidente Alfredo Cristiani, luego de seis días de diálogo en nuestra capital, constituye una victoria política para el pueblo salvadoreño, consideraron ayer miembros de la guer-rilla salvadoreña, que en horas de la mañana se reunieron con el presidente de la República, Rafael Angel Calderón, en la Casa Presidencial." See also: *La Nación*, October 29, 1992; December 17, 1992.

112 For more information concerning the peace process and the negotiations, see: *La Nación*, August 20, 1990; August 22, 1990; November 21, 1990. *Semanario Universidad* (San José, Costa Rica), July 27, 1990. *Diario Extra* (San José, Costa Rica), November 22, 1990. *La República* (San José, Costa Rica), March 3, 1995. For more informa-tion see also: Marín-Guzmán, "Al-Musahama al-Iqtisadiyya wa al-Thaqafiyya li'l-Muhajirin al-'Arab fi Amirika al-Wusta Khilal al-Qarnayn al-Tasi' 'Ashar wa al-'Ashryin", pp. 117-150. Marín-Guzmán, *A Century of Palestin-ian Immigration into Central America. A Study of Their Economic and Cultural Contributions*, passim, especially pp.42-49.

113 For more information in this respect, see: Marín-Guzmán, "Los árabes en Centroamérica", pp.462-463. See also: Marín-Guzmán, "Al-Musahama al-Iqtisadiyya wa al-Thaqafiyya li'l-Muhajirin al-'Arab fi Amirika al-Wusta Khilal

al-Qarnayn al-Tasi' 'Ashar wa al-'Ashryin", pp. 117-150. Marín-Guzmán, *A Century of Palestinian Immigration into Central America. A Study of Their Economic and Cultural Contributions*, passim, especially pp.42-49.

114 Interview with Estrella Mu'ammar, San José, Costa Rica, March 11, 1995. For more information see also: Marín-Guzmán, «El aporte económico y cultural,» passim. See also: Marín-Guzmán, "Al-Musahama al-Iqtisadiyya wa al-Thaqafiyya li'l-Muhajirin al-'Arab fi Amirika al-Wusta Khilal al-Qarnayn al-Tasi' 'Ashar wa al-'Ashryin", pp. 117-150. Marín-Guzmán, *A Century of Palestinian Immigration into Central America. A Study of Their Economic and Cultural Contributions*, passim, especially pp.42-49.

115 Interview with Suad Marcos Frech, Managua, April 19, 1995. For more information see also: Marín-Guzmán, "El aporte económico y cultural," passim. Interview with Yusuf Samara, San José, Costa Rica, January 2, 1994. Interview with Dr. 'Abd al-Fattah Sa'sa', San José, Costa Rica, October 10, 2007. Interview with Dr. 'Abd al-Fattah Sa'sa', San José, Costa Rica, June 20, 2008. Interview with' Abd al-Baqi Samara, San José, Costa Rica, January 2, 1994. For more information concerning the end of the Ottoman Empire, see: Roger Owen, *State, Power and Politics in the Making of the Modern Middle East*, Routledge, London and New York, 1992, passim, especially p. 10 and pp. 125-130. Feroz Ahmad, *The Making of Modern Turkey*, Routledge, London, 1992, passim. Bernard Lewis, *The Emergence of Modern Turkey*, Oxford University Press, London, Oxford, New York, 1968, pp. 255 ff. Peter Mansfield, *The Middle East. A Political and Economic Survey*, Oxford University Press, London, 1973, passim, especially pp. 495-499. Gustav von Grunebaum, *El Islam*, Editorial Siglo XXI, Mexico, 1981, passim.

116 Interview with Suad Marcos Frech, Managua, April 19, 1995. Interview with Dr. 'Abd al-Fattah Sa'sa', San José, Costa Rica, October 10, 2007. Interview with Dr. 'Abd al-Fattah Sa'sa', San José, Costa Rica, June 20, 2008. For more information see also: Marín-Guzmán, "Al-Musahama al-Iqtisadiyya wa al-Thaqafiyya li'l-Muhajirin al-'Arab fi Amirika al-Wusta Khilal al-Qarnayn al-Tasi' 'Ashar wa al-'Ashryin", pp. 117-150. Marín-Guzmán, *A Century of Palestinian Immigration into Central America. A Study of Their Economic and Cultural Contributions*, passim, especially pp.49-58.

117 Interview with Yusuf Samara, San José, Costa Rica, January 2, 1994. Yusuf Samara was a Palestinian immigrant to Nicaragua and a businessman who became a Nicaraguan citizen. Due to the political problems in Nicaragua during the *Sandinista* regime and the *Contras* warfare against the *Sandinista* government, Mr. Samara and his family moved to Costa Rica, where they maintain a prosperous commerce business. Mr. Yusuf Samara died back in 2008 in San José. Interview with the Palestinian-Nicaraguan poetess Suad Marcos Frech, Managua, April 19, 1995. I am indebted to my friend Christopher Boyd for all of his help in recording and transcribing much of the information in this interview with Suad Marcos Frech.

118 For more information concerning this Palestinian-Nicaraguan family see: Karla Oloscoaga D., «Suad Marcos: dos herencias y una misma causa,» in *Aljama, Revista Árabo-Centroamerica*, Vol. I, Number 2, 1990, pp. 15-16. See also: Marín-Guzmán, "El aporte económico y cultural," passim. For more details concerning the distribution of the population in Palestine see: Albert Hourani, *Minorities in the Arab World*, Oxford University Press, Oxford, 1947, pp.52-58; mainly for the distribution of the Palestinian Christian population and their economic activities. See also pp. 55-57 for the settlements of the Christian peasant population in Palestine. See also: Janet Abu-Lughod, "The demographic transformation of Palestine," in Ibrahim Abu-Lughod, *The Transformation of Palestine*, Northwestern University Press, Evanston, 1971, pp. 139-165. William Y. Adams, "Dispersed minorities of the Middle East: a comparison and a lesson," in George Pierre Castile and Gilbert Kushner, *Persistent Peoples*, University of Arizona Press, Tucson, 1981, pp. 3-25. See also: M.A. Aamir, *Jerusalem: Arab origin and heritage,* Longman, Bath, 1978, passim. M. Abir, *Local leadership and its reaction to early reforms in Palestine, 1826-1834*, Hebrew University Press, Jerusalem, 1970, passim. For more information see also: Marín-Guzmán, "Al-Musahama al-Iqtisadiyya wa al-Thaqafiyya li'l-Muhajirin al-'Arab fi Amirika al-Wusta Khilal al-Qarnayn al-Tasi' 'Ashar wa al-'Ashryin", pp. 117-150. Marín-Guzmán, *A Century of Palestinian Immigration into Central America. A Study of Their Economic and Cultural Contributions*, passim, especially pp.49-58.

119 In order to avoid confusion, the transcription of these Palestinian names has been preserved, as they were registered in the original records in Nicaragua.

120 See: Oloscoaga, «Suad Marcos,» p.15, where this poetess of Palestinian origin points out these issues. Interview with Suad Marcos Frech, Managua, April 19, 1995. Interview with Dr. 'Abd al-Fattah Sa'sa', San José, Costa Rica,

October 10, 2007. Interview with Dr. 'Abd al-Fattah Sa'sa', San José, Costa Rica, June 20, 2008. See also: Marín-Guzmán, "El aporte económico y cultural," passim. For more information see also: Marín-Guzmán, "Al-Musahama al-Iqtisadiyya wa al-Thaqafiyya li'l-Muhajirin al-'Arab fi Amirika al-Wusta Khilal al-Qarnayn al-Tasi' 'Ashar wa al-'Ashryin", pp. 117-150. Marín-Guzmán, *A Century of Palestinian Immigration into Central America. A Study of Their Economic and Cultural Contributions*, passim, especially pp.49-58.

121 Interview with Suad Marcos Frech, Managua, April 19, 1995. For more information see also: Marín-Guzmán, "El aporte económico y cultural," passim. Interview with Yusuf Samara, San José, Costa Rica, January 2, 1994. Interview with Dr. 'Abd al-Fattah Sa'sa', San José, Costa Rica, October 10, 2007. Interview with Dr. 'Abd al-Fattah Sa'sa', San José, Costa Rica, June 20, 2008.

122 Suad Marcos in the interview (Managua, April 19, 1995) pointed out that the properties the Palestinian immigrants had in this region were very small. Their agricultural production was, obviously, very limited. See also: Marín-Guzmán, «El aporte económico y cultural,» passim. For more information see also: Marín-Guzmán, "Al-Musahama al-Iqtisadiyya wa al-Thaqafiyya li'l-Muhajirin al-'Arab fi Amirika al-Wusta Khilal al-Qarnayn al-Tasi' 'Ashar wa al-'Ashryin", pp. 117-150. Marín-Guzmán, *A Century of Palestinian Immigration into Central America. A Study of Their Economic and Cultural Contributions*, passim, especially pp.49-58.

123 In order to avoid confusion, the spelling of this last name has been preserved as it was originally registred in Nicaragua.

124 Interview with Suad Marcos Frech, Managua, April 19, 1995. For more information see also: Marín-Guzmán, "El aporte económico y cultural," passim. Interview with Yusuf Samara, San José, Costa Rica, January 2, 1994. Interview with Dr. 'Abd al-Fattah Sa'sa', San José, Costa Rica, October 10, 2007. Interview with Dr. 'Abd al-Fattah Sa'sa', San José, Costa Rica, June 20, 2008.

125 Interview with Suad Marcos Frech, Managua, April 19, 1995. For more information see also: Marín-Guzmán, "El aporte económico y cultural," passim. Interview with Yusuf Samara, San José, Costa Rica, January 2, 1994. Interview with Dr. 'Abd al-Fattah Sa'sa', San José, Costa Rica, October 10, 2007. Interview with Dr. 'Abd al-Fattah Sa'sa', San José, Costa Rica, June 20, 2008.

126 In spite of its cultural interest, the *Club Árabe* in Nicaragua, as happened in other countries, had a limited range of activities and turned mainly into a center for social gatherings.

127 Interview with Suad Marcos Frech, Managua, April 19, 1995. See also: Alfredo Guzmán, "Los Nicaragüenses-Árabes," in *Aljama. Revista Arabo-Centroamericana*, Vol. I, Number 4, January, 1991, pp. 16-17, especially p. 17. See also: Moisés Hasan, " Los árabes en la vida nicaragüense," in *Aljama. Revista Arabo-Centroamericana*, Vol. I, Number 4, January, 1991, pp. 17-18. Marín-Guzmán, "El aporte económico y cultural," passim. For more information see also: Marín-Guzmán, "Al-Musahama al-Iqtisadiyya wa al-Thaqafiyya li'l-Muhajirin al-'Arab fi Amirika al-Wusta Khilal al-Qarnayn al-Tasi' 'Ashar wa al-'Ashryin", pp. 117-150. Marín-Guzmán, *A Century of Palestinian Immigration into Central America. A Study of Their Economic and Cultural Contributions*, passim, especially pp.49-58.

128 For more information concerning these issues see: Oloscoaga, «Suad Marcos,» p.15. Marín-Guzmán, "El aporte económico y cultural," passim. See also: Guzmán, "Los nicaragüenses árabes," p. 17. In this respect he wrote: "Cuando el abuelo de Jacobo Marcos envió desde Nicaragua a su hijo Jorge Jacobo Marcos Bendeck a "criase a Palestina", no se imaginó que a su regreso traería semillas de nacionalismo que fructificarían en la ideología patriótica y revolucionaria de sus nietos: Suad, Zuhayla y Jacobo Marcos Frech," (p. 17). Some Palestinian immigrants in other countries also sent their children to Palestine for their education, mainly to learn Arabic. Among the numerous examples in other regions one can mention the case of Ahmad Aburish, a Palestinian immigrant in Haiti, who after a visit to Palestine in 1946 left his children Khalil (16 years old), Daoud (14 years old) and Suleiman (12 years old) to learn Arabic. They also acquired a political conscience in defense of the Palestinian cause. For more information see: Said K. Aburish, *Children of Bethany. A story of a Palestinian family*, Indiana University Press, Bloomigton, 1988, p. 98. Aburish in this respect wrote: 'While their mastery of Arabic is far from complete they still speak an amusing, broken variety to this day," (p.98). Concerning the other issues, Aburish wrote: "His children [Ahmad Aburish's] who now live in many parts of the world, take pride in their Aburish name and shun their Haitian identity in favor of their Palestinian one. The elder, Khalil, is a committed Palestinian nationalist who devotes time and effort to the Palestinian cause." (p. 98).

129 Interview with 'Issa Frech, San José, Costa Rica, February 7, 1996. Mr. 'Issa Frech pointed out that he learned to speak Arabic, but not to read or write it. For more information see also: Marín-Guzmán, "Al-Musahama al-Iqtisadiyya wa al-Thaqafiyya li'l-Muhajirin al-'Arab fi Amirika al-Wusta Khilal al-Qarnayn al-Tasi' 'Ashar wa al-'Ashryin", pp. 117-150. Marín-Guzmán, *A Century of Palestinian Immigration into Central America. A Study of Their Economic and Cultural Contributions*, passim, especially pp.49-58.

130 For more details see: Hasan, «Los árabes en la vida nicaragüense,» p. 17. For more information see also: Marín-Guzmán, "Al-Musahama al-Iqtisadiyya wa al-Thaqafiyya li'l-Muhajirin al-'Arab fi Amirika al-Wusta Khilal al-Qarnayn al-Tasi' 'Ashar wa al-'Ashryin", pp. 117-150. Marín-Guzmán, *A Century of Palestinian Immigration into Central America. A Study of Their Economic and Cultural Contributions*, passim, especially pp.49-58.

131 Interview with Yusuf Samara, San José, Costa Rica, January 2, 1994. Interview with Suad Marcos Frech, Managua, April 19, 1995. See also: Marín-Guzmán, "El aporte económico y cultural," passim. For more information see also: Marín-Guzmán, "Al-Musahama al-Iqtisadiyya wa al-Thaqafiyya li'l-Muhajirin al-'Arab fi Amirika al-Wusta Khilal al-Qarnayn al-Tasi' 'Ashar wa al-'Ashryin", pp. 117-150. Marín-Guzmán, *A Century of Palestinian Immigration into Central America. A Study of Their Economic and Cultural Contributions*, passim, especially pp.49-58.

132 Interview with Suad Marcos Frech, Managua, April 19, 1995. Interview with Dr. 'Abd al-Fattah Sa'sa', San José, Costa Rica, October 10, 2007. Interview with Dr. 'Abd al-Fattah Sa'sa', San José, Costa Rica, June 20, 2008. See also: Marín-Guzmán, "El aporte económico y cultural," passim.

133 For more information and a detailed analysis of these issues see: Rawhi al-Khatib, *Judaization of Jerusalem*, Filastin al-Muhtalla, n.p., n.d., passim, especially pp. 16-19, and pp. 38-44. See also: Donald Neff, "Jerusalem in US policy," in *Journal of Palestine Studies*, Vol. XXIII, Number 1, (89), 1993, pp. 20-45, especially pp. 29-42. For a different interpretation, proof of the debates around these issues concerning the confiscation of Palestinian properties in Jerusalem, see also: Gideon Weigert, *Israel's presence in East Jerusalem*, Jerusalem Post Press, Jerusalem, 1973, pp. 93-95. For more information and a clear analysis of the Zionist concept of "transfer" of the Palestinian population, the abuse of power and the Israeli confiscations, see: Nur Masalha, *Expulsion of the Palestinians. The concept of "transfer" in Zionist political thought, 1882-1948*, Institute for Palestine Studies, Washington, D.C., 1993, passim. In other areas of Palestine the Israeli Government confiscated many properties of the Palestinians after the 1948 war, like in the case of the Qanawati family, whose properties were confiscated in Jerusalem, Haifa and Tel Aviv. For more information see: Interview with Michael Canavati (Qanawati), San Joaquín de Flores, Heredia, Costa Rica, March 2, 1996.

134 For more information concerning the *British Defense Regulations* and the *Emergency Regulations*, approved during the last years of the British Mandate of Palestine, see: Ann Mosely Lesch, "The Palestine Arab Nationalist Movement under the Mandate," in William B. Quandt, *The Politics of Palestinian Nationalism*, University of California Press, Berkeley, 1973, pp. 5-42. Sabri Gereis, *Les arabes en Israël*, François Maspero, Paris, 1969, passim, especially pp. 95-100. Fouzi El-Asmar, *To Be an Arab in Israel*, The Institute for Palestine Studies, Beirut, 1978, passim, especially pp. 93-94. Masalha, *Expulsion of the Palestinians*, passim, especially pp.14-38, and pp. 49-84. See also: Roberto Marín-Guzmán, *La Guerra Civil en el Líbano. Análisis del contexto político-económico del Medio Oriente*, Editorial Texto, San José, Costa Rica, 1985, Second Edition, 1986, passim, especially pp. 315-326. Roberto Marín-Guzmán, "Conflictos políticos en Palestina durante el Mandato Británico: el origen del dilema árabe-judío," in *Estudios de Asia y África*, Vol. XXII, Number 73, 1987, pp. 355-385.

135 Interview with Suad Marcos Frech, Managua, April 19, 1995. See also: Oloscoaga, «Suad Marcos,» pp. 15-16. In this interview, the poetess Suad Marcos asserted that her revolutionary position has been double, for the Palestinian cause and for the *Sandinista* revolution. She pointed out these ideas in the following words: "Yo no soy un accidente dentro de la revolución palestina. Mi formación de *Sandinista* es la que me lleva a poder manejar mi participación dentro de la Revolución Palestina." (quoted by Oloscoaga, "Suad Marcos," p. 15). For more details see also: Marín-Guzmán, "El aporte económico y cultural," passim. For more information concerning the *Sandinista* revolution and the American reaction, mainly the Reagan Administration's response against the *Sandinistas* and in favor of the *Contras*, see: Smith, *The Last Years*, pp. 185-209. See also: Peter Kornbluh, *Nicaragua: The Price of Intervention*, Institute for Policy Studies, Washington, D.C., 1987, pp. 163-165. Shultz, *Turmoil and Triumph*, passim, especially p.291, where he wrote the following lines -a good summary of the American foreign policies toward Central Amer-

ica-, in particular toward Nicaragua: "Nicaragua was at the heart of the challenge. Cuban military security advisers in Nicaragua numbered 2,000. We needed to create an atmosphere of uncertainty about our response should Cuba and the Soviets escalate their already extensive intervention. We had to take some measures to thwart Nicaragua's military support for the pro-Cuban revolutionaries in El Salvador. We had to deal with Nicaragua's diplomatic tactics, which were designed to exploit political turmoil in the United States over our Central America policy and split the United States from the other governments of Central America. I was confident that if there ever could be an honest election in Nicaragua, Ortega's government would lose. But also from our perspective, trouble at home for Ortega would decrease his ability to disrupt El Salvador and increase his willingness to negotiate a reasonable regional peace plan..." (p. 291)

136 Letter of Alvaro Herrera Martínez, Ministro Consejero (Counsellor) of the Embassy of Costa Rica in Nicaragua, Nota ECR-200-96, Managua, February 28, 1996. For more information see also: Marín-Guzmán, "Al-Musahama al-Iqtisadiyya wa al-Thaqafiyya li'l-Muhajirin al-'Arab fi Amirika al-Wusta Khilal al-Qarnayn al-Tasi' 'Ashar wa al-'Ashryin", pp. 117-150. Marín-Guzmán, *A Century of Palestinian Immigration into Central America. A Study of Their Economic and Cultural Contributions*, passim, especially pp.49-58.

137 Interview with Suad Marcos Frech, Managua, April 19, 1995. See also: Letter of Alvaro Herrera Martínez, Ministro Consejero (Counsellor) of the Embassy of Costa Rica in Nicaragua, Nota ECR-200-96, Managua, February 28, 1996. Interview with Dr. 'Abd al-Fattah Sa'sa', San José, Costa Rica, October 10, 2007. Interview with Dr. 'Abd al-Fattah Sa'sa', San José, Costa Rica, June 20, 2008. For more information see also: Marín-Guzmán, "Al-Musahama al-Iqtisadiyya wa al-Thaqafiyya li'l-Muhajirin al-'Arab fi Amirika al-Wusta Khilal al-Qarnayn al-Tasi' 'Ashar wa al-'Ashryin", pp. 117-150. Marín-Guzmán, *A Century of Palestinian Immigration into Central America. A Study of Their Economic and Cultural Contributions*, passim, especially pp.49-58.

138 Sucre Frech died on January 29, 1991. For more details see: *Aljama. Revista Arabo-Centroamericana*, Vol. I, Number 4, January 1991, p. 15. For more information see also: Marín-Guzmán, "Al-Musahama al-Iqtisadiyya wa al-Thaqafiyya li'l-Muhajirin al-'Arab fi Amirika al-Wusta Khilal al-Qarnayn al-Tasi' 'Ashar wa al-'Ashryin", pp. 117-150. Marín-Guzmán, *A Century of Palestinian Immigration into Central America. A Study of Their Economic and Cultural Contributions*, passim, especially pp.49-58.

139 See the complete text of the letter in *Aljama. Revista Arabo-Centroamericana*, Vol. I, Number 4, January 1991, p. 15. See also: Marín-Guzmán, *A Century of Palestinian Immigration into Central America*, pp.56-57.

140 For more details concerning these issues around the moving of the Embassy of Costa Rica from Tel Aviv to Jerusalem, and the political, diplomatic, and economic repercussions that it had in Costa Rica, see: Roberto Marín-Guzmán, «Nuestra Embajada en Jerusalén y sus implicaciones en la política exterior de Costa Rica,» in *Revista Estudios*, Number 5, 1984, pp.169-172. Marín-Guzmán, *La Guerra Civil en el Líbano*, pp. 296-297. Roberto Marín-Guzmán, "La Embajada de Costa Rica en Jerusalén es una burla a nuestra política de neutralidad," in *Relaciones Internacionales*, Numbers 8-9, 1984, pp. 45-51.

141 For more information concerning the internationalization of the city of Jerusalem see: 'Abd al-Hamid al-Sa'ih, *Ahammiyyat al-Quds fi al-Islam*, Wizarat al-Awqaf wa al-Shu'un wa al-Muqaddasat al-Islamiyya, 'Amman, 1979, passim. Fawzi Asadi, "Algunos elementos geográficos en el conflicto árabe-israelí," in *Estudios Árabes*, Vol. I, Number 3, 1982, pp.117-130. Roberto Marín-Guzmán, "La importancia de Jerusalén para el Islam," in *Crónica*, Number 1, 1983, pp. 72-78. Marín-Guzmán, *La Guerra Civil en el Líbano*, pp. 296-297. Roberto Marín-Guzmán, *El Islam: Ideología e Historia*, Alma Mater, Editorial de la Cooperativa de Libros de la Universidad de Costa Rica, San José, Costa Rica, 1986, passim, especially pp.123-133. Marín-Guzmán, "Conflictos políticos en Palestina," pp. 376-378. Roger Louis, *The End of the Mandate in Palestine*, University of Texas Press, Austin, Texas, 1988, passim. Neff, "Jerusalem in US policy," passim, especially pp. 21-24.

142 Information provided by Lic. Mario Rodríguez, Ministry of Foreign Affairs, Nicaragua, quoted in Letter of Alvaro Herrera Martínez, Ministro Consejero (Counsellor) of the Embassy of Costa Rica in Nicaragua, Nota ECR-200-96, Managua, February 28, 1996. Interview with Dr. 'Abd al-Fattah Sa'sa', San José, Costa Rica, August 1, 2008. See also: Marín-Guzmán, "Los árabes en Centroamérica", p.470.

143 Interview with Oscar Bakit, the son of Zacarías Bakit, San José, Costa Rica, November 30, 1994. Oscar Bakit studied law and advertising at The University of Costa Rica. In 1949 he obtained his Ph. D. in law, at Universidad

de Granada, Granada, Nicaragua. See also: Interview with Oscar Bakit, San José, Costa Rica, February 8, 1996. Interview with Doreen Bakit, daughter of Oscar Bakit, San José, Costa Rica, February 26, 1996. Interview with Dr. 'Abd al-Fattah Sa'sa', San José, Costa Rica, October 10, 2007. Interview with Dr. 'Abd al-Fattah Sa'sa', San José, Costa Rica, June 20, 2008.

144 Interview with Oscar Bakit, San José, Costa Rica, February 8, 1996. Interview with Dr. 'Abd al-Fattah Sa'sa', San José, Costa Rica, October 10, 2007. Interview with Dr. 'Abd al-Fattah Sa'sa', San José, Costa Rica, June 20, 2008.

145 Interview with Mayra Hasbun, daughter of 'Isa Ibrahim (Salvador Abraham) Hasbun Hasbun, San José, Costa Rica, February 15, 1996. Interview with Warde (Rosa) Hasbun Dabdoub, San José, Costa Rica, February 17, 1996. See also: Interview with Mayra Hasbun, San José, Costa Rica, February 17, 1996.

146 Interview with Mayra Hasbun, San José, Costa Rica, February 17, 1996. See also: Marín-Guzmán, «El aporte económico y cultural,» passim. For more information see also: Marín-Guzmán, "Al-Musahama al-Iqtisadiyya wa al-Thaqafiyya li'l-Muhajirin al-'Arab fi Amirika al-Wusta Khilal al-Qarnayn al-Tasi' 'Ashar wa al-'Ashryin", pp. 117-150. Marín-Guzmán, *A Century of Palestinian Immigration into Central America. A Study of Their Economic and Cultural Contributions*, passim, especially pp.59-81.

147 Interview with Mayra Hasbun, San José, Costa Rica, February 15, 1996. Interview with Mayra Hasbun, San José, Costa Rica, February 17, 1996. See also: Interview with Warde (Rosa) Hasbun Dabdoub, San José, Costa Rica, February 17, 1996. Interview with Dr. 'Abd al-Fattah Sa'sa', San José, Costa Rica, October 10, 2007. Interview with Dr. 'Abd al-Fattah Sa'sa', San José, Costa Rica, June 20, 2008. For more information see also: Marín-Guzmán, "Al-Musahama al-Iqtisadiyya wa al-Thaqafiyya li'l-Muhajirin al-'Arab fi Amirika al-Wusta Khilal al-Qarnayn al-Tasi' 'Ashar wa al-'Ashryin", pp. 117-150. Marín-Guzmán, *A Century of Palestinian Immigration into Central America. A Study of Their Economic and Cultural Contributions*, passim, especially pp.59-81.

148 Interview with Mayra Hasbun, San José, Costa Rica, February 15, 1996. Interview with Dr. 'Abd al-Fattah Sa'sa', San José, Costa Rica, October 10, 2007. Interview with Dr. 'Abd al-Fattah Sa'sa', San José, Costa Rica, June 20, 2008.

149 Interview with Mayra Hasbun, San José, Costa Rica, February 15, 1996. See also: Marín-Guzmán, «El aporte económico y cultural,» passim.

150 The Hasbun family still owns this sawmill in the province of Limón. William Hasbun, a son of Salvador Abraham Hasbun Hasbun, administrated this business for many years. See: Interview with Mayra Hasbun, San José, Costa Rica, February 15, 1996. See also: Marín-Guzmán, "El aporte económico y cultural," passim. For more information see also: Marín-Guzmán, "Al-Musahama al-Iqtisadiyya wa al-Thaqafiyya li'l-Muhajirin al-'Arab fi Amirika al-Wusta Khilal al-Qarnayn al-Tasi' 'Ashar wa al-'Ashryin", pp. 117-150. Marín-Guzmán, *A Century of Palestinian Immigration into Central America. A Study of Their Economic and Cultural Contributions*, passim, especially pp.59-81.

151 Interview with Dr. 'Abd al-Fattah Sa'sa', San José, Costa Rica, December 23, 1993. Doctor 'Abd al-Fattah Sa'sa' immigrated in Costa Rica in 1973. He is originally from Jaffa and studied gynecology in Spain and in Costa Rica. He resides in San José and has become a Costa Rican citizen. Interview with Oscar Bakit, San José, Costa Rica, November 30, 1994. Interview with Estrella Mu'ammar, San José, Costa Rica, March 11, 1995. Interview with Dr. 'Abd al-Fattah Sa'sa', San José, Costa Rica, October 10, 2007. Interview with Dr. 'Abd al-Fattah Sa'sa', San José, Costa Rica, June 20, 2008. See also: Marín-Guzmán, "El aporte económico y cultural," passim. For more information see also: Marín-Guzmán, "Al-Musahama al-Iqtisadiyya wa al-Thaqafiyya li'l-Muhajirin al-'Arab fi Amirika al-Wusta Khilal al-Qarnayn al-Tasi' 'Ashar wa al-'Ashryin", pp. 117-150. Marín-Guzmán, *A Century of Palestinian Immigration into Central America. A Study of Their Economic and Cultural Contributions*, passim, especially pp.59-81.

152 Interview with Ivonne Hasbun, daughter of 'Isa (Salvador) Jorge Hasbun, San José Costa Rica, February 23, 1996. Ivonne Hasbun taught Grammar School for over thirty years in different schools in the province of Cartago. For more information see also: Marín-Guzmán, "Al-Musahama al-Iqtisadiyya wa al-Thaqafiyya li'l-Muhajirin al-'Arab fi Amirika al-Wusta Khilal al-Qarnayn al-Tasi' 'Ashar wa al-'Ashryin", pp. 117-150. Marín-Guzmán, *A Century of Palestinian Immigration into Central America. A Study of Their Economic and Cultural Contributions*, passim, especially pp.59-81.

153 Interview with Ivonne Hasbun, San José, Costa Rica, February 23, 1996, and also San José, Costa Rica, August 12, 1996. Interview with Dr. 'Abd al-Fattah Sa'sa', San José, Costa Rica, October 10, 2007. Interview with Dr. 'Abd al-Fattah Sa'sa', San José, Costa Rica, June 20, 2008.

154 Interview with Ivonne Hasbun, San José, Costa Rica, February 23, 1996. For more information see also: Marín-Guzmán, "Al-Musahama al-Iqtisadiyya wa al-Thaqafiyya li'l-Muhajirin al-'Arab fi Amirika al-Wusta Khilal al-Qarnayn al-Tasi' 'Ashar wa al-'Ashryin", pp. 117-150. Marín-Guzmán, *A Century of Palestinian Immigration into Central America. A Study of Their Economic and Cultural Contributions*, passim, especially pp.59-81.

155 Interview with Ivonne Hasbun, San José, Costa Rica, February 23, 1996. Interview with Dr. 'Abd al-Fattah Sa'sa', San José, Costa Rica, October 10, 2007. Interview with Dr. 'Abd al-Fattah Sa'sa', San José, Costa Rica, June 20, 2008. For more information see also: Marín-Guzmán, "Al-Musahama al-Iqtisadiyya wa al-Thaqafiyya li'l-Muhajirin al-'Arab fi Amirika al-Wusta Khilal al-Qarnayn al-Tasi' 'Ashar wa al-'Ashryin", pp. 117-150. Marín-Guzmán, *A Century of Palestinian Immigration into Central America. A Study of Their Economic and Cultural Contributions*, passim, especially pp.59-81.

156 Interview with Ivonne Hasbun, San José, Costa Rica, February 23, 1996. For more information see also: Marín-Guzmán, "Al-Musahama al-Iqtisadiyya wa al-Thaqafiyya li'l-Muhajirin al-'Arab fi Amirika al-Wusta Khilal al-Qarnayn al-Tasi' 'Ashar wa al-'Ashryin", pp. 117-150. Marín-Guzmán, *A Century of Palestinian Immigration into Central America. A Study of Their Economic and Cultural Contributions*, passim, especially pp.59-81.

157 Interview with Oscar Bakit, San José, Costa Rica, November 30, 1994. See also: Marín-Guzmán, "El aporte económico y cultural," passim. For more information see also: Marín-Guzmán, "Al-Musahama al-Iqtisadiyya wa al-Thaqafiyya li'l-Muhajirin al-'Arab fi Amirika al-Wusta Khilal al-Qarnayn al-Tasi' 'Ashar wa al-'Ashryin", pp. 117-150. Marín-Guzmán, *A Century of Palestinian Immigration into Central America. A Study of Their Economic and Cultural Contributions*, passim, especially pp.59-81.

158 Both Universities are located in San José. Interview with Mayra Hasbun, San José, Costa Rica, February 15, 1996. Interview with Dr. 'Abd al-Fattah Sa'sa', San José, Costa Rica, October 10, 2007. Interview with Dr. 'Abd al-Fattah Sa'sa', San José, Costa Rica, June 20, 2008. See also: Marín-Guzmán, "El aporte económico y cultural," passim.

159 For more details see: *Colección de Leyes, Decretos, Acuerdos y Resoluciones*, Imprenta Nacional, San José, Costa Rica, 1904, pp. 308-309. This decree was based on Law number 6, of May 22, 1897, and it says: *"ASCENSIÓN ESQUIVEL Presidente Constitucional de la República de Costa Rica, considerando: Que es urgente que el Gobierno dicte medidas preventivas para evitar la inmigración de gentes que por su raza, sus hábitos de vida y su espíritu aventurero e inadaptable a un medio ambiente de orden y de trabajo, serían en el país motivo de degeneración fisiológica y elementos propicios para el desarrollo de la holganza y del vicio. Por tanto, De conformidad con el artículo 2 de la ley número 6 del 22 de mayo de 1897 y sin perjuicio de lo en ella dispuesto con respecto a los individuos de raza amarilla, Decreta:* Artículo 1- Prohíbese el ingreso a la República de árabes, turcos, sirios, armenios y gitanos de cualquier nacionalidad. Artículo 2- Los Capitanes de puerto, al practicar la visita sanitaria de cada nave, tomarán nota, con vista de los papeles respectivos, de la raza y la nacionalidad de los individuos á quienes alcance la calificación del artículo anterior, les comunicará sin demora la prohibición de desembarcar, dando de ello noticia al propio tiempo al Capitán del barco. Artículo 3- En tal caso, el funcionario comunicará lo ocurrido al Gobernador del lugar, para hacer efectiva la prohibición y aún ampararla por los medios de la ley, si fuere necesario. Dado en la ciudad de San José, a los diez días del mes de Junio de mil novecientos cuatro. Ascensión Esquivel. El Secretario de Estado en el Despacho de Policía. José Astúa Aguilar." See also: Marín-Guzmán, "El aporte económico y cultural," passim.

160 Interview with Dr. 'Abd al-Fattah Sa'sa', San José, Costa Rica, December 27, 1993. Interview with Oscar Bakit, San José, Costa Rica, November 30, 1995. Interview with Doreen Bakit, San José, Costa Rica, February 26, 1996. Alberto Bakit spoke fluently eleven languages. When asked for the reasons he learned so many languages, answered that it was "because Palestine is the knot of all roads", and also "because Palestine is the center of all routes." For more information see: Interview with Oscar Bakit, San José, Costa Rica, February 8, 1996. Interview with Dr. 'Abd al-Fattah Sa'sa', San José, Costa Rica, October 10, 2007. Interview with Dr. 'Abd al-Fattah Sa'sa', San José, Costa Rica, June 20, 2008. See also: Marín-Guzmán, "El aporte económico y cultural," passim. For more information see also: Marín-Guzmán, "Al-Musahama al-Iqtisadiyya wa al-Thaqafiyya li'l-Muhajirin al-'Arab fi Amirika al-Wusta

Khilal al-Qarnayn al-Tasi' 'Ashar wa al-'Ashryin", pp. 117-150. Marín-Guzmán, *A Century of Palestinian Immigration into Central America. A Study of Their Economic and Cultural Contributions*, passim, especially pp.59-81.

161 Interview with Dr. 'Abd al-Fattah Sa'sa', San José, Costa Rica, December 27, 1993. Interview with Oscar Bakit, San José, Costa Rica, November 30, 1995. Interview with Estrella Mu'ammar, San José, Costa Rica, March 11, 1995. Interview with Dr. 'Abd al-Fattah Sa'sa', San José, Costa Rica, October 10, 2007. Interview with Dr. 'Abd al-Fattah Sa'sa', San José, Costa Rica, June 20, 2008. See also: Marín-Guzmán, "El aporte económico y cultural," passim.

162 Interview with Dr. 'Abd al-Fattah Sa'sa', San José, Costa Rica, February 21, 1995. Interview with Dr. 'Abd al-Fattah Sa'sa', San José, Costa Rica, February 4, 1996. Interview with Dr. 'Abd al-Fattah Sa'sa', San José, Costa Rica, October 10, 2007. Interview with Dr. 'Abd al-Fattah Sa'sa', San José, Costa Rica, June 20, 2008. For more information see also: Marín-Guzmán, "Al-Musahama al-Iqtisadiyya wa al-Thaqafiyya li'l-Muhajirin al-'Arab fi Amirika al-Wusta Khilal al-Qarnayn al-Tasi' 'Ashar wa al-'Ashryin", pp. 117-150. Marín-Guzmán, *A Century of Palestinian Immigration into Central America. A Study of Their Economic and Cultural Contributions*, passim, especially pp.59-81.

163 Interview with 'Issa Frech, San José, Costa Rica, February 7, 1996. Hanna Frech, a Palestinian immigrant, arrived to Nicaragua in 1954. He was also the owner of a clothing factory in Managua from 1978 to 1983. Due to the political problems in Nicaragua during the 1980s Hanna Frech left Nicaragua for Panama in 1983. In 1994 he and his son, 'Issa Frech, moved to Costa Rica, where they reside now. It is important to point out that Hanna Frech became Muslim. His sons also adopted the faith of Islam, following their father's example. However, Hanna Frech's daughters remained Christians. Interview with Dr. 'Abd al-Fattah Sa'sa', San José, Costa Rica, February 21, 1995. Interview with Dr. 'Abd al-Fattah Sa'sa', San José, Costa Rica, February 4, 1996. Interview with Dr. 'Abd al-Fattah Sa'sa', San José, Costa Rica, October 10, 2007. Interview with Dr. 'Abd al-Fattah Sa'sa', San José, Costa Rica, June 20, 2008. See also: Marín-Guzmán, "El aporte económico y cultural," passim. Interview with 'Issa Frech, San José, Costa Rica, February 7, 1996.

164 Interview with 'Issa Frech, San José, Costa Rica, February 7, 1996.

165 Interview with Oscar Bakit, San José, Costa Rica, February 8, 1996. Mr. Oscar Bakit died in San José, Costa Rica, on July 25, 1998.

166 Interview with Michael Canavati (Qanawati), San Joaquín de Flores, Heredia, Costa Rica, March 2, 1996. See also: Marín-Guzmán, «El aporte económico y cultural,» passim. Michael Qanawati was born in Bethlehem and emigrated first to Honduras in 1957, after the Suez Crisis of 1956. Later on he lived with his family in United States for fourteen years, and finally moved to Costa Rica on May 12, 1974. He resides in Escazú, a neighborhood of San José.

167 Interview with Michael Canavati (Qanawati), San Joaquín de Flores, Heredia, Costa Rica, March 2, 1996. See also: Marín-Guzmán, «El aporte económico y cultural,» passim. For more information see also: Marín-Guzmán, "Al-Musahama al-Iqtisadiyya wa al-Thaqafiyya li'l-Muhajirin al-'Arab fi Amirika al-Wusta Khilal al-Qarnayn al-Tasi' 'Ashar wa al-'Ashryin", pp. 117-150. Marín-Guzmán, *A Century of Palestinian Immigration into Central America. A Study of Their Economic and Cultural Contributions*, passim, especially pp.59-81.

168 Interview with Michael Canavati (Qanawati), San Joaquín de Flores, Heredia, Costa Rica, March 2, 1996. For more information see also: Marín-Guzmán, "Al-Musahama al-Iqtisadiyya wa al-Thaqafiyya li'l-Muhajirin al-'Arab fi Amirika al-Wusta Khilal al-Qarnayn al-Tasi' 'Ashar wa al-'Ashryin", pp. 117-150. Marín-Guzmán, *A Century of Palestinian Immigration into Central America. A Study of Their Economic and Cultural Contributions*, passim, especially pp.59-81.

169 For more details see: Interview with Jihad Abed, San José, Costa Rica, February 21, 1995. Interview with Dr. 'Abd al-Fattah Sa'sa', San José, Costa Rica, February 4, 1996. Interview with Dr. 'Abd al-Fattah Sa'sa', San José, Costa Rica, October 10, 2007. Interview with Dr. 'Abd al-Fattah Sa'sa', San José, Costa Rica, June 20, 2008. See also: Marín-Guzmán, "El aporte económico y cultural," passim.

170 Interview with Halima Samara, San José, Costa Rica, February 20, 1996. Interview with Flora Marín de Sa'sa', Dr. 'Abd al-Fattah Sa'sa's wife, San José, Costa Rica, May 14, 1996. See also: Interview with Dr. 'Abd al-Fattah Sa'sa', San José, Costa Rica, October 10, 2007. Interview with Dr. 'Abd al-Fattah Sa'sa', San José, Costa Rica, June 20, 2008.

171 Interview with 'Abd al-Karim Tahir, San José, Costa Rica, March 25, 1995, and also: Interview with 'Abd al-Karim Tahir, San José, Costa Rica, April 1, 1995. Interview with Dr. 'Abd al-Fattah Sa'sa', San José, Costa Rica, February 4, 1996. For more information see also: Marín-Guzmán, "Al-Musahama al-Iqtisadiyya wa al-Thaqafiyya li'l-Muhajirin al-'Arab fi Amirika al-Wusta Khilal al-Qarnayn al-Tasi' 'Ashar wa al-'Ashryin", pp. 117-150. Marín-Guzmán, *A Century of Palestinian Immigration into Central America. A Study of Their Economic and Cultural Contributions*, passim, especially pp.59-81.

172 Interview with Dr. 'Abd al-Fattah Sa'sa', San José, Costa Rica, February 4, 1996. Interviews with Flora Marín de Sa'sa', San José, Costa Rica, May 14, 1996, and June 1, June 5 and June 19, 1996. Interview with Dr. 'Abd al-Fattah Sa'sa', San José, Costa Rica, October 10, 2007. Interview with Dr. 'Abd al-Fattah Sa'sa', San José, Costa Rica, June 20, 2008.

173 Interview with Kamal Rishmawi, San José, Costa Rica, March 13, 1995. Interview with 'Abd al-Karim Tahir, San José, Costa Rica, March 25, 1995, and also: Interview with 'Abd al-Karim Tahir, San José, Costa Rica, April, 1995. Interview with Dr. 'Abd al-Fattah Sa'sa', San José, Costa Rica, February 4, 1996. Interviews with Flora Marín de Sa'sa', San José, Costa Rica, May 14, 1996 and June 1, June 5 and June 19, 1996. Interview with Dr. 'Abd al-Fattah Sa'sa', San José, Costa Rica, October 10, 2007. Interview with Dr. 'Abd al-Fattah Sa'sa', San José, Costa Rica, June 20, 2008. See also: Marín-Guzmán, "El aporte económico y cultural," passim.

174 Interview with Fernando Guardia Alvarado, functionary of the Ministry of Foreign Affairs of Costa Rica, who also occupied the positions of Costa Rican Ambassador to Dominican Republic (1990-1992) as well as to Argentina (1992-1994). San José, Costa Rica, February 24, 1995. Later Mr. Guardia Alvarado was appointed Costa Rican Ambassador to Paraguay (1998-2002, and 2002-2006). See also: Interview with Dr. 'Abd al-Fattah Sa'sa', San José, Costa Rica, February 4, 1996. Marín-Guzmán, «El aporte económico y cultural,» passim.

175 For more information see: Interview with Doreen Bakit, San José, Costa Rica, February 26, 1996. Interview with Dr. 'Abd al-Fattah Sa'sa', San José, Costa Rica, October 10, 2007. Interview with Dr. 'Abd al-Fattah Sa'sa', San José, Costa Rica, June 20, 2008. See also: Marín-Guzmán, "El aporte económico y cultural," passim.

176 Interview with Doreen Bakit, San José, Costa Rica, February 26, 1996. See also: Interview with Doreen Bakit, San José, Costa Rica, March 4, 1996. For more information see also: Marín-Guzmán, "Al-Musahama al-Iqtisadiyya wa al-Thaqafiyya li'l-Muhajirin al-'Arab fi Amirika al-Wusta Khilal al-Qarnayn al-Tasi' 'Ashar wa al-'Ashryin", pp. 117-150. Marín-Guzmán, *A Century of Palestinian Immigration into Central America. A Study of Their Economic and Cultural Contributions*, passim, especially pp.59-81.

177 Palestinian immigrants, Christians as well as Muslims, and also those in Palestine who did not emigrate, have been always interested in education. Education has been the way to excel. As examples see the descriptions of the Aburish family in Bethany in: Aburish, *Children*, pp. 138 ff., and El-Asmar family, in El-Asmar, *To Be an Arab in Israel,* passim. See also: Nevill Barbour, *Nisi Dominus. A survey of the Palestine controversy*, The Institute for Palestine Studies, Beirut, 1969, passim, especially pp. 124-129, where he explains the Arab and Jewish education systems during the British Mandate. Despite the numerous efforts to improve the Arab education in Palestine, "this, however, was rapidly curtailed on account of "lack of funds"; and throughout the Mandatory regime expenditure on education has formed a far lower percentage of the total expenditure than it has in Iraq or Egypt," (Barbour, *Nisi Dominus*, p. 128.) Even the Royal Commission (The Peel Commission) in 1936 reported: "The expansion of Arab educational services has up to now barely kept pace with the expansion of the school-age population, and it will have to be increased considerably if any radical improvement in the extent of education is to be effected," quoted by Barbour, *Nisi Dominus*, p. 128. It has been demonstrated that in the formation of the modern states in the Middle East -influenced and as a result of European colonialism- two thirds of the total expenditure was on security. The British Mandate of Palestine was not an exception in this process. For more details see: Owen, *State, Power and Politics*, pp. 15-16, where he wrote: "A last important feature of the administrative system established in the colonial period was their particular emphasis on police and security. No doubt this is a feature of all new states. But in the case of the colonial power it was, for obvious reasons, considered to be the key to continued political control. This can easily be seen by an examination of the budgets of the period in which, typically, some two-thirds of total expenditure was security related... Most of this was spent in creating and developing a police force and, perhaps also, a rural gendarmerie. Less importance was attached to a local army, partly for financial reasons, partly because

the colonial power itself accepted the major responsibility for external defense. Nevertheless, small military formations of a few thousand men or so were organized in all colonial states, and even though they were given few heavy weapons and were used mainly for internal security, patterns of recruitment and politization were established which were to play a significant role in the immediate post-independence period... Such emphasis on security left little money for education, public health and welfare, although enough was still spent on secondary schools and technical institutes to produce a growing number of activist youths who were willing recruits into the first anti-colonial movements of the 1920s and 1930s." (pp. 15-16).

178 Interview with Dr. 'Abd al-Fattah Sa'sa', San José, Costa Rica, January 4, 1994. Interviews with Flora Marín de Sa'sa', San José, Costa Rica, May 14, 1996 and June 1, June 5 and June 19, 1996. Interview with Dr. 'Abd al-Fattah Sa'sa', San José, Costa Rica, October 10, 2007. Interview with Dr. 'Abd al-Fattah Sa'sa', San José, Costa Rica, June 20, 2008. See also: Marín-Guzmán, "El aporte económico y cultural," passim. It is also important to mention that recently many more Arab immigrants have arrived to Costa Rica, from different countries in the Arab World: Egypt, Libya, 'The United Arab Emirates, Algeria, and Iraq. This proves the continued movement of Arab populations from the Middle East and North Africa to Costa Rica, as well as to other countries in Central America. Many of them have arrived to Costa Rica due to their marriages to Costa Ricans. They have devoted themselves to various activities: some are merchants; others have small farms for coffee production; few others teach (philosophy and an Iraqi who died in 2010 taught journalism) at the Universidad de Costa Rica. Some others are women married to Costa Ricans and nowadays are housewives.

179 For more information see: González, *Dollar*, passim, especially p. 96. See also: Marín-Guzmán, "El aporte económico y cultural," passim.

180 See: González, *Dollar*, p. 173. See also: Marín-Guzmán, "El aporte económico y cultural," passim. For more information see also: Marín-Guzmán, "Al-Musahama al-Iqtisadiyya wa al-Thaqafiyya li'l-Muhajirin al-'Arab fi Amirika al-Wusta Khilal al-Qarnayn al-Tasi' 'Ashar wa al-'Ashryin", pp. 117-150. Marín-Guzmán, *A Century of Palestinian Immigration into Central America. A Study of Their Economic and Cultural Contributions*, passim, especially pp.82-83.

181 See: *El Guatemalteco*, LXXIX, Number 25, Guatemala City, Guatemala, January 15, 1914. I am indebted to my colleague at the University of Costa Rica, Dr. Arturo Taracena, for providing me this information. For more details see also: Marín-Guzmán, "Al-Musahama al-Iqtisadiyya wa al-Thaqafiyya li'l-Muhajirin al-'Arab fi Amirika al-Wusta Khilal al-Qarnayn al-Tasi' 'Ashar wa al-'Ashryin", pp. 117-150. Marín-Guzmán, *A Century of Palestinian Immigration into Central America. A Study of Their Economic and Cultural Contributions*, passim, especially pp.82-83.

182 Information provided by Guatemalan historian José Cal Montoya, professor at the Universidad San Carlos de Guatemala. Letter dated August 13, 2008, p.1. See also: Marín-Guzmán, "Los árabes en Centroamérica", p.478. For more information see also: Marín-Guzmán, "Al-Musahama al-Iqtisadiyya wa al-Thaqafiyya li'l-'Arab fi Amirika al-Wusta Khilal al-Qarnayn al-Tasi' 'Ashar wa al-'Ashryin", pp. 117-150. Marín-Guzmán, *A Century of Palestinian Immigration into Central America. A Study of Their Economic and Cultural Contributions*, passim, especially pp.82-83.

183 For more details see: Roberto Marín-Guzmán, «Las causas de la emigración libanesa durante el siglo XIX y principios del siglo XX. Un estudio de historia económica y social,» in *Estudios de Asia y África*, Vol. XXXI, Number 3 (101), September-December 1996, pp. 557-606. See also: Deniz Akarli, "Ottoman attitudes towards Lebanese emigration, 1885-1910," in Albert Hourani and Nadim Shehadi, *The Lebanese in the World: A Century of Emigration*, The Center of Lebanese Studies, London, 1992, pp. 109-138. See also: Albert Hourani, *Arabic Thought in the Liberal Age, 1798-1939*, Cambridge University Press, Cambridge, 1983, passim, especially pp. 25-33 and pp. 55-66. For more details concerning the remittances to Mount Lebanon, for example, and the great impact they had in this country, see the letter that Naum Pasha, governor of Mount Lebanon, sent to the Ottoman Minister of the Interior, dated Sha'ban 16, 1312 (February, 1895), quoted by Akarli, "Ottoman Attitudes," p. 122, which says: "Most of Mount Lebanon is rocky; and uncultivable land. Mulberry trees constitute its principle plantation, and silk production the major source of income for the Lebanese in general. The continuous decline of silk prices over the last years, however, multiplied the difficulties which Lebanese encounter in maintaining their sustenance. The

stringent conditions in Mount Lebanon contrast sharply with the opportunities of making a much better living abroad... Under the circumstances, the Lebanese become eager to try their fortunes overseas... They do not intend to settle in America and do not see any advantage in changing their citizenship, because they fully appreciate the privileges they enjoy... [within the Ottoman system] and the comprehensive compassion His Majesty the Sultan feels for them. They go abroad to work and return home with the money they earn after a few years. In this way, a significant amount of cash has already entered [the Lebanese economy], as witnessed by the sharp increase in real estate prices and the signs of prosperity in many villages and towns." For more details see also: Roberto Marín-Guzmán, *La Emigración Libanesa en los Siglos XIX Y XX. Análisis de sus Causas Económico-Sociales*, Alma Mater, Cooperativa de Libros de la Universidad de Costa Rica, San José, Costa Rica, 1997, passim, especially pp. 108-121.

184 As a general pattern in this process it is also possible to notice that the same, that has been explained for the last Palestinian immigrants can also be observed as a general characteristic of the last Arab immigrants, mainly from North Africa. For more details see: Marín-Guzmán, "El aporte económico y cultural," passim. Marín-Guzmán, "Los inmigrantes árabes en México," passim. Marín-Guzmán, "Al-Muhajirun al-'Arab fi al-Maksik Khilal al-Qarnayn al-Tasi' 'Ashar wa al-'Ashryin", pp.93-116. Zéraoui, "Los árabes en México," passim. Alfaro-Velcamp, *So Far from Allah so Close to Mexico. Middle Eastern Immigrants in Modern Mexico*, passim. Marín-Guzmán and Zéraoui, *Arab immigration in Mexico in the Nineteenth and Twentieth centuries. Assimilation and Arab heritage*, passim. Roberto Marín-Guzmán, "Nuevos aportes para el estudio de los inmigrantes árabes en México, siglos XIX-XXI", in *Estudios de Asia y África*, Vol. XLIV, Número 1 (138), 2009, pp.135-171. Marín-Guzmán, *A Century of Palestinian Immigration into Central America. A Study of Their Economic and Cultural Contributions*, passim, especially pp.82-83.

185 A shorter version of this work was published in *Journal of Palestine Studies. See* Manzar Foroohar, "Palestinians in Central America: From Temporary Emigrants to a Permanent Diaspora," *Journal of Palestine Studies,* Vol. XL, No. 3 (Spring 2011), pp. 6-22, ISSN: 0377-919X; electronic ISSN: 1533-8614.

186 While the history of Palestinian immigration to the United States, Mexico, and South America has been the subject of major scholarly investigations, the communities in Central America have received very little scholarly attention.

187 According to Amaya Banegas, Palestinians make up 90 percent of Honduras's Arab population. Jorge Alberto Amaya Banegas, *Los Árabes y Palestinos en Honduras (1900-1950)* (Tegucigalpa: Editorial Guaymuras, 1997), p. 74.

188 See William K. Crowley, "San Pedro Sula, Honduras: The Order and Disorder of the Pubescent Period in Central America's most Rapidly Growing City." (PhD diss., University of Oregon, Department of Geography, 1972); Nancie Gonzáles, *Dollar, Dove and Eagle, One Hundred Years of Palestinian Migration to Honduras.* (Ann Arbor: The University of Michigan Press, 1992); and Dario A. Euraque, "The Arab-Jewish Economic Presence in San Pedro Sula, the Industrial Capital of Honduras: Formative Years, 1880-1930s." *Immigrants and Minorities* (March-July 1997), p. 107.

189 Najib E. Saliba, "Emigration from Syria," in *Arabs in the New World*, eds. Sameer Y. Abraham and Nabeel Abraham (Detroit: Wayne State University, Center for Urban Studies, 1983), p. 38; Kemal H. Karpat, "The Ottoman Emigration to America, 1860-1914." *International Journal of Middle East Studies,* 17, no. 2 (May 1985):175-209; and Akram Fouad Khater, *Inventing Home, Emigration, Gender, and the Middle Class in Lebanon, 1870-1920* (Berkeley/Los Angeles/London: University of California Press, 2001), p. 49.

190 As Ignacio Klich noted, "General conscription into the Ottoman armed forces was first introduced in 1855. At the time, Christian opposition resulted in them being exempted from service; like the Jews, Christians paid a tax for this privilege. Following the Young Turks' take-over, though, such a concession was abolished." See Ignacio Klich, "Criollos and Arabic Speakers in Argentina: An Uneasy *Pas de Deux,* 1888-1914," in *The Lebanese in the World: A Century of Emigration,* eds. Albert Hourani and Nadim Shehadi (London: The Center for Lebanese Studies in association with I. B. Tauris, 1992), pp. 243-84, p. 247.

191 Author's interviews with Fahmy Hassan, Managua, 27 June 2008; Julia Dabdub, Bethlehem, 15 April 2008; Nader Abu Amsha, Beit Sahur, 4 April 2008; Adnan Musallam, Bethlehem, 31 March 2008; Hanna Shokri Yusef Mitri, Bethlehem, 5 April 2008; and George Samour, Bethlehem, 29 March 2008

192 Philip K. Hitti, *The Syrians in America*, Gorgias Press, 2005, p. 57.

193 Saliba, "Emigration from Syria,"p. 38; and Karpat, "The Ottoman Emigration to America," p. 179.

194 Author's interview with Nader Abu Amsha, Beit Sahur, 4 April 2008.

195 María Cruz Burdiel de las Heras, *La emigración Libanesa en Costa Rica* (Madrid: CantArabia, 1991), p. 29.

196 Author's interview with Fehmy Hassan, Managua, 27 June 2008; Hanna Shokri Yusef Mitri, Bethlehem, 5 April 2008; Florence Hasbun Saca, San Salvador, 1 July 2007; and Rosita Hasbun Zaid de Nasser, San Salvador, 2 July 2007.

197 Interview with Fehmy Hassan, 27 Managua, June 2008.

198 Philip K. Hitti, *The Syrians in America*, p. 48.

199 Saliba, "Emigration From Syria," p. 36.

200 Adnan A. Musallam, "In Search of Stability and Opportunities: Early Palestinian Immigration to Latin America and Problems Encountered." Unpublished paper presented at the Middle East Conference, California State University, Fresno, Oct. 16-18, p. 11. Also author's interview with Mrs. Julia Dabdub, Bethlehem, 5 April 2008; and Nader Abu Amsha, Beit Sahur, 4 April 2008.

201 Roberto Marín Guzman,"El Aporte Económico y Cultural de la Inmigración Árabe en Centroamérica en los Siglos XIX y XX," in *El Mundo Árabe y América Latina*, ed. Lorenzo Agar Corbinos and Raymundo Kabchi (Madrid: UNESCO, 1997), p. 164.

202 Dario Euraque, "The Arab-Jewish Economic Presence in San Pedro Sula," p. 107.

203 Jorge Alberto Amaya Banegas, *Los Árabes Y Palestinos en Honduras,* p. 49.

204 Roberto Marín Guzman believes that about 15% to 20% of Palestinian immigrants to Honduras were Muslim Palestinians who did not declare their religion or converted to Christianity after arrival in Honduras. He could only account for 17 Muslim families in Honduras in the 1990s. See Marín Guzman, "El Aporte Económico y Cultural de Inmigración," p. 167. Moisés Hassan's father, Ahmed Musa Hassan, was also a Muslim Palestinian who arrived in Nicaragua around 1916-17. He married a Catholic Nicaraguan woman, Maria Elsa Morales, and his children were baptized in the Catholic Church. (Author's interview with Moisés Hassan (Issa Moisés Hassan Morales), Managua, 26 June 2008.)

205 See Marín Guzman, "El Aporte Económico"; and Crowley, *San Pedro Sula: Honduras: The Order and Disorder*.

206 Author's Interviews with Julia Dabdoub, Bethlehem, 5 April 2008; Adnan Musallam, Bethlehem, 31 March 2008; Nader Abu Amsha, Beit Sahur, 4 April 2008; Anton Salim Jadallah Zidan, Beit Jalla, 5 April 2008; Linda Jabra Jeris Hadweh, Beit Jalla, 5 April 2008; Jack Giacaman, Bethlehem, 1 April 2008; and Hanna Shokri Yusef Mitri, Bethlehem, 5 April 2008.

207 The Ottoman Empire introduced public education only in the latter part of the 19th century. It was based on the French system and Turkish translation of French text books. Since the medium was Turkish, it failed to attract the majority of Arab-speaking Palestinians. In addition to public schools, many private Islamic religious schools taught mostly boys in reading and writing Arabic. See Ismael Abu-Saad and Duane Champagne, "Introduction: A Historical Context of Palestinian Arab Education," *The American Behavioral Scientist*, 49 (April 2006), pp. 1035-51.

208 Edward Hagopian and A.B. Zahlan, "Palestine's Arab Population: The Demography of the Palestinians,": in *Journal of Palestine Studies*, 3, no. 4 (Summer 1974), pp. 32-73, p. 38.

209 Ibid.

210 Dario A. Euraque, "The Arab-Jewish Economic Presence in San Pedro Sula, the Industrial Capital of Honduras: Formative Years, 1880-1930s," p. 108.

211 See William K. Crowley, "The Levantine Arabs: Diaspora in the New World," *Proceedings of the Association of American Geographers*, VI (1974): 140. Also see Bukele Kattn, *Palestina, Tierra Santa, Historia, Emigración, Influencia Cultural* (San Salvador, circa 2005), 8.

212 Honduras, especially the city of San Pedro Sula is the home of the largest Palestinian community in Central America. In the early 1990s, Nancie Gonzalez estimated that Palestinian immigrants and their descendants make up "about one-forth of the population of 350,000 who live in San Pedro Sula." Gonzalez, *Dollar, Dove and Eagle, One Hundred Years of Palestinian Migration to Honduras*, p. 10. Dario Euraque estimates Palestinian population in Honduras around 170,000.

213 See Antonio Murga Frassinetti, "The Liberal Reform," in Nancy Peckenham and Annie Street (eds.) *Honduras Portrait of a Captive Nation.* New York: Praeger Publishers, 1985: 29-33, P. 32.

214 Amaya Benegas, *Los Árabes Y Palestinos en Honduras*, pp. 63-64.

215 Dario A. Euraque, "The Arab-Jewish Presence in San Pedro Sulla," p. 110.

216 Amaya Banegas, *Los Árabes Y Palestinos en Honduras*, p. 80.

217 Amaya Banegas, *Los Árabes Y Palestinos en Honduras*, p. 81.

218 Euraque, *Merchants and Industrialists in Northern Honduras*, p. 115.

219 Amaya Banegas, *Los Árabes Y Palestinos en Honduras*, pp. 121-122.

220 Euraque, *Merchants and Industrialists in Northern Honduras*, p. 197.

221 Amaya Banegas, *Los Árabes Y Palestinos en Honduras*, p. 122.

222 Amaya Banegas, *Los Árabes Y Palestinos en Honduras,* pp. 135-136.

223 Euraque, *Merchants and Industrialists in Northern Honduras,* p. 257 (footnote #81).

224 Ibid., p. 258 (footnote # 82).

225 Larry Luxner, "Honduras: Palestinian Success Story," *Latinamerica Press* (July 16, 2001).

226 Bukele Kattan, *Palestina, Tierra Santa, Historia, Emigración, Influencia Cultural*, p. 8.

227 See Roberto Marin Guzman, "El Aporte Económico y Cultural de Inmigración," pp. 177-178.

228 Interview with Claudio Hasbun, San Salvador, 29 June 2007.

229 Euraque, *Merchants and Industrialists in Northern Honduras,* p. 258.

230 Amaya Banegas, *Los Árabes Y Palestinos en Honduras,* p. 89.

231 Euraque, *Merchants and Industrialists in Northern Honduras: The Making of a National Bourgeoisie in Peripheral Capitalism*, p. 254.

232 *El Cronista*, Tegucigalpa, 4 March 1922, cited in Marvin Barahona, *Evolución histórica de la identidad nacional* (Tegucigalpa: Editorial Guaymuras, 1991), p. 244.

233 *La Gaceta,* Tegucigalpa, No. 7.995, Tegucigalpa, 11 September 1929.

234 See Euraque, *Merchants and Industrialists in Northern Honduras*, p. 256.

235 The number of Salvadorans of Palestinian ancestry has been estimated at 90,000. See Matt Horton, "Shafik Giries Abdullah Handal (1930-2006)," *Washington Report on Middle East Affairs* (April 2006), pp. 42-43.

236 Patricia Parkman, *Nonviolent Insurrection in El Salvador: The Fall of Maximiliano Hernández Martínez* (Tucson: The University of Arizona Press, 1988), 21.

237 Poder Legislativo, Decreto número 39 (24 July 1941) Art. 4, *Diario Oficial,* República de El Salvador, San Salvador, Numero 174 (9 August 1941).

238 Ignacio Klich, "Latin America, the United States and the Birth of Israel: The Case of Somoza's Nicaragua," *Journal of Latin American Studies*, 20, No. 2. (Nov. 1988), 417-418, footnote # 45.

239 Decreto No. 6, El Congreso Constitucional de la República de Costa Rica, 20 May 1897, *Colección de las Leyes, Decretos y Órdenes Expedidos por los Supremos Poderes Legislativo y Ejecutivo de Costa Rica*, 70-71.

240 *Colección de las Leyes, Decretos y Órdenes Expedidos por los Supremos Poderes Legislativo y Ejecutivo de Costa Rica (1904),* 308.

241 Patricia Alvarenga Venutolo, "La inmigración extranjera en la historia Costarricense," in *El Mito Roto, Inmigración y Emigración en Costa Rica,* ed. Carlos Sándobal G. (San José, Costa Rica: Editorial UCR, Instituto de Investigaciones Sociales, 2007), 14-15.

242 Marín Guzman, "El Aporte Económico y Cultural de la Inmigración," p. 189.

243 Author's interview with Dr. Abd al-Fatah Sa'sa, San José, Costa Rica, 1 July 2008.

244 Amaya Banegas, *Los Árabes Y Palestinos en Honduras,* p. 84.

245 Author's interview with Armando Bukele Kattan, San Salvador, 3 July 2007; Humberto Bukele Kattan, San José, Costa Rica, 30 June 2008; Jeaneth Burbara de Abusulef, Beit Sahur, 8 April 2008.

246 Bukele Kattan, *Palestina, Tierra Santa, Historia, p. 11.*

247 Larry Luxner, "Honduras: Palestinian Success Story," Latinamerica Press (16 July 2001).

248 ARENA was founded in 1988 by Roberto D'Aubuisson, a known organizer and leader of Salvadoran death squads responsible for killing of thousands of civilians, including Archbishop Oscar Romero.

249 Schafik Giries Abdullah Handal was born on 14 October 1930, in Usulután, El Salvador, in a large family of Palestinian Catholic merchants who had migrated from Bethlehem to El Salvador in the 1920s. He became a political activist at an early age. In the 1950s, when he was studying at the university, he joined the outlawed Communist Party.

250 Johanna Tuckman, "Schafik Handal, Guerrilla leader in El Salvador's civil war," The Guardian, (February 17, 2006).

251 Author's interview with Florence Hasbun, San Salvador, 1 July 2007.

252 Tuchman, "Schafik Handal."

253 Author's nterview with Jorge Schafik Handal Vega (son of Schafik Handal), San Salvador, 3 July 2007.

254 At present, there are probably roughly 500 families of Palestinian origin in Nicaragua.

255 Author's interview with Moisés Hassan in Manauga, 26 June 2008 and Moisés Hassan's email message to the author, 9 July 2008.

256 Ibid.

257 Ibid.

258 Author's interview with Suad Marcos Frech, Managua, 25 June 2008.

259 Author's interview with Nader Abu Amsha, Bait Sahur, 4 April 2008; Isa Muslih, Bait Sahur, 30 March 2008; and George Samour, Bethlehem, 29 March 2008.

260 Amaya Banegas, *Los Árabes y Palestinos en Honduras (1900-1950), p* . 92.

261 Gonzalez, *Dollar, Dove and Eagle, One Hundred Years of Palestinian Migration to Honduras*, pp. 138-139.

262 Roberto Marín Guzman, "El Aporte Económico y Cultural de la Inmigración," p. 175.

263 Ibid., p. 182. Palestinian immigrants in other Central American countries established similar clubs. In Nicaragua, for example, they established *Club Árabe* on 15 May 1958. The Club was a gathering place for all Arabs of Nicaragua, although about 80% of its members were Palestinians.

264 Author's interviews with Claudio Hasbun, San Salvador 29 June 2007; Florance Hasbun, San Salvador1 July 2007; John Nasser Hasbun, San Salvador, 1 July 2007; Dr. Amar Mustafa Radi, Guatemala City, 6 June 2007; Amy Janet Handal, San Pedro Sula, 8 July 2007; and Fahmy Hassan, Managua, 27 June 2008.

265 Gonzalez, *Dollar, Dove, and Eagle*, p. 163.

266 Author's interviews with Fahmy Hassan, Managua, 27 June 2008; Johny Hazbun, Guatemala City, 23 June 2007; Dr. Amar Mustafa Radi, Guatemala City, 6 June 2007; Dr. Abd al-Fattah Sa'sa, San José, Costa Rica, 1 July 2008; Armando Bukele Kattan, San Salvador, 3 July 2007.

267 Author's interview with Dr. Abd al-Fattah Sa'sa, San José, Costa Rica, 1 July 2008.

268 Marín Guzman, "El Aporte Económico y Cultural de la Inmigración," pp. 189-190.

269 Author's interview with Dr. Abd al-Fattah Sa'sa, San José, Costa Rica, 1 July 2008.

270 Author's interview with Jorge Schafik Handal Vega, San Salvador, 3 July 2007.

271 Horton, "Schafik Giries Abdullah Handal," pp. 42-43.

272 Gonzalez, *Dollar, Dove, and Eagle,* pp. 79-80.

273 Author's interview with John Nasser Hasbun, San Salvador, 1 July 2007. John Nasser Hasbun was the main force behind the building of the two commemorative plazas for Palestine in San Salvador. His passion for social justice, as demonstrated in his work in the ranks of the FMLN, and his dedication to his roots in Palestine were major factors in my decision to write this article. Despite his poor health, he decided to visit Palestine for the first time in October 2007. Upon his return to San Salvador he died in January 2008 from a long illness. At his funeral, his casket was wrapped in both Salvadoran and Palestinian flags.

274 Sarah, 1970, p. 15

275 Acevedo, 2005, p. 16

276 Agar, 2009

277 Agar, 2009

278 Acevedo, 2005, p. 7

279 Agar and Rebolledo, 1997

280 Nasser, 2006, p. 12

281 Agar, 1983

282 Samamé, 2006

283 Olguín and Peña, 1990, p. 140-141

284 Allél, 1937, p. 35

285 Agar and Rebolledo, 1997

286 Agar, 2009

287 Olguín and Peña, 1991, p. 93

288 Allél, 1937

289 Olguín and Peña, 1991, p. 92

290 Acevedo, 2005, p. 7

291 Agar and Rebolledo, 1997

292 Nasser, 2006, p.12

293 These refugees arrive to Chile as a product of a humanitarian resettlement act, through an agreement between the High Commissioner of the United Nations and the Government of Chile. The majority of these people were born on Iraqi soil, but they left the country fleeing persecution from which they were victim to after the fall of Saddam Hussein.

294 Agar, 2009

295 Agar and Saffie, 2009

296 Allél, 1937, P. 32 - 33

297 Allél, 1937, P. 34

298 Allél, 1937

299 Allél, 1937, p. 37

300 Agar and Saffie, 2005

301 Olguín and Peña, 1990, p. 100

302 Olguín and Peña 1990, p. 100 - 101

303 Agar and Saffie, 2005

304 Agar, 2009

305 Agar, 2009

306 Agar and Saffie, 2009

307 Ruiz and Saiz , 2006, p. 342

308 Ruiz and Saiz, 2006, p. 7

309 Ruiz and Saiz , 2006, p. 8

310 Ruiz and Saiz , 2006, p. 343

311 Agar and Saffie, 2005

312 Acevedo, 2005, p. 25

313 Agar and Saffie, 2005, p. 17

314 Touzri, 2008, p. 59

315 Higher-income sector of Santiago.

316 On the outskirts of the capital.

317 Acevedo, 2005, p. 25

318 Agar, 2009

319 Typical [Arabic] food

320 Ruiz and Saiz, 2006, p. 341

321 Olguín and Peña, 1990, p. 95

322 Agar and Saffie, 2005, p. 8

323 Daher, 1986, p.76

324 Daher, 1986

325 Agar, 2009

326 Based on the authors' own estimates.

327 Chile's Government statement on the recognition of a Palestinian State. Retrieved January 10th, 2011, from www. gob.cl/informa/2011/01/07/declaracion-del-gobierno-de-chile-sobre-reconocimiento-del-estado-de-palestina.htm
328 Acevedo, 2005, p.8
329 Agar and Saffie, 2005
330 Agar and Saffie, 2005, p. 14
331 Agar, 2009
332 Typical Arabic dishes.
333 Agar, 2009
334 Touzri, 2008, p. 86
335 Agar, 2009
336 Touzri, 2008, p. 88
337 Agar and Saffie, 2009

Bibliography:

Sisters and Brothers in the Diaspora:Palestinian Christians in Latin America

- David Sheinin, Lois Baer Barr (ed.), *The Jewish Diaspora in Latin America: New Studies on History and Literature*, Graland Publishing, New York & London, 1996.

- Doris Musalem Rahal „La migración palestina a México, 1893-1949" in: „*Destino México : un estudio de las migraciones asiáticas a México siglos XIX y XX*" , El Colegio de México, Centro de Estudios de Asia y Africa, 1997, pp. 305-355.

- Fu'ad Farah, *The Living Stones: The Arab Christians in the Holy Land,* Nazareth, 2003.

- Jamil Safady, *A cultura Arabe no Brasil, Libano e Síria*, São Paulo, 1972.

- Jeffrey Lesser, Ignacio Klich, *Arab and Jewish Immigrants in Latin America: Images and Realities,* London, Frank Cass, 1998.

- Jorge Safady, *Antologia Arabe do Brasil,* São Paulo: Editora Safady, 1973.

- Judith Laikin Elkin, Gilbert W. Merkx (ed.) *The Jewish Presence in Latin America*, Allen & Unwin, Boston, 1987.

- Kemal H. Karpat, *Studies on Ottoman social and political history: selected articles and essays*, Brill, 2002.

- Leyla Bartet,Farid Kahhat *La huella árabe en el Perú, Congreso de la República, 2010.*

- Maria Narbona, *Islam and Muslims in Latin America: An Overview*, Florida International University, April 2010.

- Nancie L. González, *One Hundred Years of Palestinian Migration to Honduras,* Dollar, Dove, and Eagle, Ann Arbor: The University of Michigan Press, 1992.

- Nancie L. Gonzalez,Carolyn S. McCommon (ed.) „The Christian Palestinians of Honduras: an uneasy accommodation" in: *Conflict, migration, and the expression of ethnicity*, Boulder, Westview Press, 1989.

- Olivier Prud'homme, "Los Cristianos de la region de Euphrata (Palestina) y sus practicas comerciales en el Salvador entre 1886 y 1918", *VIII Congreso Centroamericano de Historia*, Antigua, Guatemala, 2006.

- Pedro Brieger , Enrique Herszkowich, "The Muslim Community of Argentina," in: *The Muslim World* [Hartford], 92, no. 1, 2 Spring 2002, pp. 157-68.

- Peter Beyer, B. Clarke Peter, *The World´s Religions: Continuities and Transformations,* London: Routledge 2009.

- Rania Al Qass Collings, Rifat Odeh Kassis, Mitri Raheb (ed.) *Palestinian Christians Facts, Figures and Trends 2008*, Diyar, Bethlehem 2008.

- Raymond Delval, *Les musulmans en Amérique Latine et aux Caraibes*, París: Editions L'Harmattan, 1992.

- Robert M. Levine, *Tropical Diaspora, The Jewish Experience in Cuba*, University Press of Florida, Gainesville 1993.

- Roberto Marín-Guzmán, *A Century of Palestinian Immigration into Central America: A Study of Their Economic and Cultural Contributions*", Editorial Universidad de C.R, 2000.

- Roberto Marin-Guzman, Zeraoui Zidane, *Arab Immigration in Mexico in the Nineteenth and Twentieth Centuries: Assimilation and Arab Heritage*, Augustine Press & Instituto Tecnologico de Monterrey, Monterrey, 2003.

- Rosa Araya Suazo, *La iglesia ortodoxa en chile. patriarcado de antioquia y todo el oriente*, Master thesis at the Facultad de Filosofia y Educacibn, Centro de Estudios Arabes, Universidad de Chile, Santiago, 1986.

- Sari Hanafi, "Rethinking the Palestinians Abroad as a Diaspora: The relationship between the Diaspora and the Palestinian Territories" in: Andreh Levi, Alex Weingrod, *Homelands and Diasporas: Holy Lands and Other Places*, Stanford University Press 2005, pp. 97-122.

- Victor A. Mirelman, *Jewish Buenos Aires 1890-1930. In Search of an Identity,* Detroit: Wayne State University Press, 1990.

- Waltraut Kokot, Khachig Tölölyan, Carolin Alfonso (eds.), *Diaspora, Identity and Religion. New Directions in Theory and Research*, London, New York, Routledge 2004.

Online Resources:

- Orthodox Archbishop of Chile. Retrieved on April, 12th, 2012, from http://www.chileortodoxo. cl/arqui.html

A Century of Palestinian Immigration to Chile: A Successful Integration

- Ahmad Hassan Mattar, *Guía social de la colonia árabe en Chile (siria, palestina, libanesa) [Arabic Community Social Guide in Chile (Syrian, Palestinian, Lebanese)]*. Santiago, Chile: Ahués Brothers Editorial, 1941.

- Daniela Lahsen, *Construcción de una nueva identidad chilena-palestina* [Construction of a New Chilean-Palestinian Identity]. Graduate Thesis, Bachelors of History, Universidad Finis Terrae, Santiago, Chile, 2001.

- Lorenzo Agar, "Inmigrantes y descendientes de árabes en Chile: adaptación social" [Arab

Immigrants and Descendants in Chile: Social Adjustment]: in Abdeluahed Akmir (coordinator), *Los árabes en América Latina. Historia de una emigración* [Arabs in Latin America. History of Emigration]. Madrid, Spain: Siglo XXI, 2009, pp. 99-170.

- Lorenzo Agar, Nicole Saffie, "Chilenos de origen Árabe: la Fuerza de las Raíces" [Chileans of Arab Origin: The Strength of the Roots]: in *Revista Miscelánea de Estudios Árabes y Hebraicos*, Sección Árabe-Islam (Universidad de Granada), Vol. 54, 2005, pp. 3-27.

- Lorenzo Agar, Antonia Rebolledo, "La inmigración árabe en Chile: los caminos de integración" [Arab Immigration in Chile: The Roads to Integration]: in *El mundo árabe y América Latina* [The Arab World and Latin America]. Madrid, Spain: UNESCO / Libertarian / Proudhufi, 1997, pp. 283-309.

- Lorenzo Agar, "El comportamiento urbano de los migrantes árabes en Chile" [Urban Behavior of Arab Migrants in Chile] (Electronic versión): in *Eure*, 9 (27), 1983, pp. 73-84.

- Marco Allél, *Las industrias de las colectividades de habla árabe en* Chile [The factories of Arabic-speaking communities in Chile]. Santiago, Chile: Syrian-Palestinian Business Association, 1937.

- María Olga Samamé, "La poesía del mahyar o de la emigración árabe a Chile y a Colombia, a través de los poetas Mahfud Massís y Jorge García Ustá" [Mahyar Poetry or Arab Emigration to Chile and Colombia, through the Massif Mahfud Poets and Jorge García Ustá]: in *Taller de Letras*, Pontificia Universidad Católica de Chile, 39, 2006, pp. 9-24.

- María Teresa Daher, *Exploración psicosocial de la inmigración libanesa en Chile* [Psychosocial Exploration of the Lebanese Immigration to Chile]. Graduate Thesis, Psychology, Catholic University of Chile, Santiago, Chile, 1986.

- Mercedes Del Amo, "La literatura de los periódicos árabes de Chile" [The Literature of the Arab Newspapers in Chile]: in *MEAH, Arabic-Islam Section*, 55, 2006, pp. 3-35.

- Myriam Olguín, Patricia Peña, *La inmigración árabe en Chile* [Arab Immigration to Chile]. Santiago, Chile: Ed. Instituto Chileno-Árabe de Cultura, 1990.

Patricia Acevedo et al, Informe Patronato. Núcleo de Antropología Urbana "Historias, Trayectorias e Imaginarios Urbanos de los Habitantes de la Ciudad de Santiago: 1950-2000" [Patronato Report. Urban Anthropology Core "Histories, Trajectories and Urban Imagery of the Inhabitants of Santiago: 1950-2000]. Fondecyt 1050031. Santiago, Chile, 2005.

- Roberto Sarah, *Los turcos* [The Turks]. Santiago, Chile: Obre Editorial, 1970.

- Rosa María Ruiz Moreno, Guadalupe Sáiz Muñoz, "Visión de género en dos periódicos de la comunidad árabe en Chile (años treinta)" [Gender perspective in two Arab community newspapers in Chile (1930's)]: in *MEAH*, Arabic-Islam Section, 55, 2006, 339-378.

- Sundus Nasser, *La emigración de los Palestinos a América Latina, con especial atención en la emigración a Chile* [The Emigration of Palestinians to Latin America, with Special Attention to the Emigration to Chile]. Graduate Thesis, Multilingual Communication, Fachhochschule Köln (Cologne University of Applied Sciences), Cologne, Germany, 2006.

- Sonia Touzri, *La integración socioespacial de los inmigrantes árabes en Chile [Socio-spatial Integration of Arab Immigrants in Chile]*. Research seminar, Supérieure Ecole Nationale Belleville exchange program - Faculty of Architecture and Planning University of Chile, Santiago, Chile, 2008.

- Others:
  - Orthodox Archbishop of Chile. Retrieved on December 21st, 2010, from http://www.chileortodoxo.cl/arqui.html

Selected Bibliography

- Ahmad Tarabin, "Aspects of Syrian Arab Emigration to the United States,": in *Damascus University Journal*, Vol.2, June 1985 (in Arabic).

- Ahmad Hassan Mattar, *Guía social de la colonia árabe en Chile (siria, palestina, libanesa)*, Santiago, Chile, Ahués Brothers Editorial, 1941.

- Abdeluahed Akmir, *Los Árabes en América Latina. Historia de una emigración*, Casa Árabe, Siglo XXI, Madrid, 2009.

- Aby Kaufman, Yoram Shapira, "Jews and Arabs in Latin America": in *Patterns of Prejudice*, Vol.10, no.1, January–February 1976, pp. 15-26.

- Adnan Musallam, "A Nation of Immigrants: The Arab Immigrant Experience in America", Curriculum Development Center (Outreach Program), Center for Near Eastern and North African Studies, The University of Michigan, Ann Arbor, Michigan, 1981.

- Akram Fouad Khater, *Inventing Home, Emigration, Gender, and the Middle Class in Lebanon, 1870-1920*, Berkeley/Los Angeles/London: University of California Press, 2001.

- Al-Badawi al-Mulatham, *Arabic Speakers in South America* , part one, Beirut 1956 (in Arabic).

- Albert Hourani and Nadim Shehadi (eds.) *The Lebanese in the World, A Century of Emigration*, The Centre for Lebanese Studies, London 1992.

- Ayyub Musalam, "Pages from the Book: Bethlehem in the Depth of History and as Described by Travellers and Historians": in *Bait Lahm* (The Antonian Society Bulletin), Vol.2, 1987 (in Arabic).

- Charles Issawi, *An Economic History of the Middle East and North Africa*, New York, 1982.

- Clair Price, "Bethlehem under the British", in: *The Living Age*, Vol. 305, no. 3962, June 20, 1920.

- Daniela Lahsen, *Construcción de una nueva identidad chilena-palestina*, Graduate Thesis, Bachelors of History, Universidad Finis Terrae, Santiago, Chile 2001.

– Darío A. Euraque, "Los árabes en Honduras: entre la inmigración, la acumulación y la política": in *Contribuciones Árabes a las Identidades Iberoamericanas*, Casa Árabe, Madrid, 2009, pp. 233-284.

– Dario A. Euraque, "The Arab-Jewish Economic Presence in San Pedro Sula, the Industrial Capital of Honduras: Formative Years, 1880-1930s,": in *Immigrants and Minorities* (March-July 1997).

– David Adams, "Los "Turcos" de Honduras,": in *Aljama.* Revista Arabo-Centroamericana, Vol. I, Number 3, September-December, 1990, pp.12-14.

– Donald W. Bray, "The political emergence of Arab-Chileans, 1952-1958 ": in *Journal of Inter-American Studies*, Vol. IV, no.4, oct. 1962.

– Doris Musalem Rahal "La migración palestina a México, 1893-1949" in: María Elena Ota Mishima, editor, *Destino México : un estudio de las migraciones asiáticas a México siglos XIX y XX* , El Colegio de México, Centro de Estudios de Asia y Africa, 1997, pp. 305-355.

– Fu'ad Farah, *The Living Stones: The Arab Christians in the Holy Land*, Nazareth, 2003 (in Arabic).

– Giries Elali, *Bethlehem, The Immortal town*, Bethlehem, 1991.

– Ignacio Klich, "Criollos and Arabic Speakers in Argentina: An Uneasy Pas de Deux, 1888-1914": in Albert Hourani and Nadim Shehadi (eds.), *The Lebanese in the World: A Century of Emigration*, The Center for Lebanese Studies in association with I. B. Tauris, London, 1992, pp. 243-84.

– Ignacio Klich, Jeffrey Lesser, "Introduction: 'Turco' inmigrants in Latin America": in *The Americas*, Vol.53, no.1, 1996, pp.1-14.

– Jamil Safady , *A cultura Arabe no Brasil, Libano e Síria* ,São Paulo, 1972.

– Jeffrey Lesser, "(Re)creating ethnicity: Middle Eastern Immigration to Brazil": in *The Americas*,Vol.53, no.1, 1996, pp.45-65.

– Jeffrey Lesser, Ignacio Klich , *Arab and Jewish Immigrants in Latin America: Images and Realities*, Frank Cass, London, 1998.

– Jorge Alberto Amaya Banegas, *Los árabes y palestinos en Honduras, 1900-1950*, editorial Guaymuras, Tegucigalpa, Honduras, 2000.

– Jorge Safady , *Antologia Arabe do Brasil*, São Paulo: Editora Safady, 1973.

– Juan Abugattas, "The Perception of the Palestinian Question in Latin America ": in *Journal of Palestinian Studies*, Vol.11, no. 3, Spring 1982, pp. 117-128.

– Judith Laikin Elkin, Gilbert W. Merkx (ed.) *The Jewish Presence in Latin America*, Allen & Unwin, Boston, 1987.

– Kemal H. Karpat, "The Ottoman Emigration to America, 1860-1914": in *International Journal of Middle East Studies*, Vol. XVII , no. 2, May 1985, pp. 175-209.

– Kemal H. Karpat, *Studies on Ottoman social and political history: selected articles and essays*, Brill, 2002.

– Leyla Bartet,Farid Kahhat, *La huella árabe en el Perú* , Congreso de la República, 2010.

– Lorenzo Agar, "Inmigrantes y descendientes de árabes en Chile: adaptación social": in Abdeluahed Akmir (coordinator), *Los árabes en América Latina. Historia de una emigración*, Madrid, Spain: Siglo XXI, 2009, pp. 99-170.

– Lorenzo Agar, " El comportamiento urbano de los migrantes árabes en Chile" (Electronic versión): in *Eure*, 9 (27), 1983, pp. 73-84.

– Lorenzo Agar (ed.), *Encuesta a la población de origen árabe en Santiago de Chile (EPOA)*,Santiago de Chile (inédito), 2001.

– Lorenzo Agar, "El comportamiento urbano de los migrantes árabes en Chile": in *Eure*, Santiago, Vol. 11, no. 27, 1983, pp. 73-74.

– Lorenzo Agar, Antonia Rebolledo, "La inmigración árabe en Chile: los caminos de laintegración": in *El Mundo Árabe y América Latina*, Ediciones UNESCO/Libertarias/Prodhufi, Paris, 1997, pp. 283-309.

– Lorenzo Agar, Nicole Saffie, "Chilenos de origen Árabe: la Fuerza de las Raíces",: in *Revista Miscelánea de Estudios Árabes y Hebraicos, Sección Árabe-Islam* (Universidad de Granada), Vol. 54, 2005 pp. 3-27.

– Mercedes Del Amo, " La literatura de los periódicos árabes de Chile": in *MEAH*, Arabic-Islam Section, 55, 2006, pp. 3-35.

– María Olga Samamé , " La poesía del mahyar o de la emigración árabe a Chile y a Colombia, a través de los poetas Mahfud Massís y Jorge García Ustá": in *Taller de Letras*, 39, 2006, pp. 9-24.

– María Olga Samamé, "Transculturación, identidad y alteridad en novelas de la inmigración árabe hacia Chile": in *Signos*, 2003, Vol.36, no.53, pp.51-73.

– Myriam Olguín, Patricia Peña, *La inmigración árabe en Chile*, Santiago, Chile: Ed. Institute Chilean-Arab Culture, 1990.

– María Teresa Daher, *Exploración psicosocial de la inmigración libanesa en Chile*. Graduate Thesis, Psychology, Catholic University of Chile, Santiago, Chile, 1986.

– Marcos Martínez, "Los hondureños de origen árabe": in *Aljama*. Revista Arabo-Centroamericana, Vol. I, no. 3, September-December, 1990, pp. 15-16.

– María Cruz Burdiel de las Heras, *La emigración Libanesa en Costa Rica*, Madrid: CantArabia, 1991

- Maria Narbona, *Islam and Muslims in Latin America: An Overview*, Florida International University, April 2010.

- Mario Posas, "La Plantación Bananera en Centro América (1870-1929)": in Víctor Hugo Acuña, *Historia General de Centro América*, Vol. IV "Las Repúblicas Bananeras", FLACSO, San José, 1994, pp.111-165.

- Mike George Salman, "Emigration and its effect on the extinction of Bethlehem familie" : in *Al-Liqa'*, 4th Year, Vol. 1, 1989 (in Arabic).

- Monica Almeida, "Phoenicians of the Pacific: Lebanese and other Middle Easterners in Ecuador": in *The Americas*, Vol.53, no. 1, 1996, pp. 87-111.

- Najib E. Saliba, "Emigration from Syria": in Sameer Y. Abraham and Nabeel Abraham (eds.), *Arabs in the New World: Studies in Arab-American Communities*, Detroit: Wayne State University Center for Urban Studies, 1983, pp. 30-43.

- Nancie L. González "One Hundred Years of Palestinian Migration to Honduras", Dollar, Dove, and Eagle, Ann Arbor: The University of Michigan Press, 1992.

- Nancie L. Gonzalez,Carolyn S. McCommon (ed.) "The Christian Palestinians of Honduras: an uneasy accommodation" in: *Conflict, migration, and the expression of ethnicity*, Boulder , Westview Press, 1989, pp. 75-90.

- Nellie Ammar, "They came from the Middle East": in *Jamaica Journal*, Vol. IV, Number 1, 1970, pp. 2-6

- Olivier Prud'homme, "Los Cristianos de la region de Euphrata (Palestina) y sus practicas comerciales en el Salvador entre 1886 y 1918", *VIII Congreso Centroamericano de Historia*, Antigua, Guatemala, 2006.

- Pedro Brieger , Enrique Herszkowich, "The Muslim Community of Argentina" in: *The Muslim World* [Hartford], 92, No. 1, 2 (Spring 2002), pp. 157-68.

- Peter Beyer, B. Clarke Peter, *The World's Religions: Continuities and Transformations*, London, Routledge 2009.

- Philip Hitti, *History of Syria, Lebanon and Palestine*, Vol.2, Translated by Kamal al-Yazigi, Beirut 1959 (in Arabic).

- Philip Hitti, *Arabs. A Short History*, Gateways Editions, London, 1965.

- Philip K. Hitti, *The Syrians in America*, Gorgias Press, 2005.

- Rosa María Ruiz Moreno, Guadalupe Sáiz Muñoz, "Visión de género en dos periódicos de la comunidad árabe en Chile (años treinta)": in *MEAH*, Arabic-Islam Section, 55, 2006339-378.

- Roberto Sarah, *Los turcos* , Santiago, Chile: Obre Editorial, 1970.

- Rania Al Qass Collings, Rifat Odeh Kassis, Mitri Raheb (eds.), *Palestinian Christians Facts, Figures and Trends 2008*, Diyar, Bethlehem 2008.

- Raymond Delval, *Les musulmans en Amérique Latine et aux Caraibes*, París: Editions L'Harmattan, 1992.

- Roberto Marín-Guzmán, *A Century of Palestinian Immigration into Central America: A Study of Their Economic and Cultural Contributions*, Editorial Universidad de C.R, 2000.

- Roberto Marín-Guzmán, Zidane Zéraoui, *Arab immigration in Mexico in the Nineteenth and Twentieth centuries. Assimilation and Arab heritage*, Augustin Press and Instituto Tecnológico de Monterrey, Austin, Texas and Monterrey, Mexico, 2003.

- Roberto Marín-Guzmán, " Los inmigrantes árabes en México en los siglos XIX Y XX. Un estudio de historia social, ": in Raymundo Kabchi, El Mundo Árabe y América Latina, Ediciones UNESCO y Libertarias, Madrid, 1997, pp. 123-154.

- Roberto Marín-Guzmán, "Al-Muhajirun al-'Arab fi al-Maksik Khilal al-Qarnayn al-Tasi' 'Ashar wa al-'Ashryin": in 'Abd al-Wahid Akmir, (ed.), *Al-Watan al-'Arabi wa Amirika al-Latiniyya*, Markaz Dirasat al-Wahda al-'Arabiyya, Beirut, 2005, pp.93-116.

- Roberto Marín-Guzmán, "Al-Musahama al-Iqtisadiyya wa al-Thaqafiyya li'l-Muhajirin al-'Arab fi Amirika al-Wusta Khilal al-Qarnayn al-Tasi': in *'Ashar wa al-'Ashryin"*, pp. 117-150.

- Rosa Araya Suazo, *La iglesia ortodoxa en chile. patriarcado de antioquia y todo el oriente*, Master thesis at the Facultad de Filosofia y Educacibn, Centro de Estudios Arabes, Universidad de Chile, Santiago, 1986.

- Sonia Touzri, *La integración socioespacial de los inmigrantes árabes en Chile* [Socio-spatial Integration of Arab Immigrants in Chile]. Research seminar, Supérieure Ecole Nationale Belleville exchange program - Faculty of Architecture and Planning University of Chile, Santiago, Chile, 2008.

- Sameer Y. Abraham and Nabeel Abraham (eds.), *Arabs in the New World: Studies in Arab-American Communities*, Detroit: Wayne State University Center for Urban Studies, 1983.

- Sari Hanafi, "Rethinking the Palestinians Abroad as a Diaspora: The relationship between the Diaspora and the Palestinian Territories" in: Andreh Levi, Alex Weingrod, *Homelands and Diasporas: Holy Lands and Other Places*, Stanford University Press 2005, pp. 97-122.

- Sundus Nasser, *La emigración de los Palestinos a América Latina, con especial atención en la emigración a Chile* [The Emigration of Palestinians to Latin America, with Special Attention to the Emigration to Chile]. Graduate Thesis, Multilingual Communication, Fachhochschule Köln (Cologne University of Applied Sciences), Cologne, Germany, 2006.

- Theresa Alfaro-Velcamp, *So Far from Allah, so Close to Mexico. Middle Eastern Immigrants in Modern Mexico*, University of Texas Press, Austin, Texas, 2007.

– Victoria Kattan de Hirmas, *Mis 100 años de vida: Chilena nacida en Belén*, A&V Ed., Santiago, 2005

– Walid Rabi', "Emigration and Alienation in Palestinian Society, a Folkloric Social Study", in: *Society and Heritage*, Number 3, Vol.1, October 1974, (in Arabic).

– Waltraut Kokot, Khachig Tölölyan, Carolin Alfonso (eds.), *Diaspora, Identity and Religion. New Directions in Theory and Research*, London; New York, Routledge, 2004.

– William K. Crowley, "The Levantine Arabs: Diaspora in the New World,": *in Proceedings of the Association of American Geographers*, Number 6, 1974, pp. 137-142.

– Zidane Zeraoui, "Los arabes en México: El Perfil de la Migracion" In: María Elena Ota, *Destino México: un estudio de las migraciones asiaticas a México, siglos XIX y XX*, México, El Colegio de México, 1997, pp.252-282.

– Zidane Zéraoui, "Los árabes en México: entre la integración y el arabismo,": in *Revista Estudios*, Numbers 12-13, 1995-1996, pp. 13-39.

Biographies

Viola Raheb

Was born in 1969 in Bethlehem, Palestine. She obtained her master's degree in Education and Evangelical Theology from the Ruprecht-Karl University in Heidelberg, Germany. She began her career in formal and informal education in 1995. She was the Deputy Schools' Director of the Evangelical Lutheran Schools in Jordan and Palestine from 1995 to 1998, and managed the Public Relations Department of the International Center of Bethlehem. From 1998–2002 she headed the educational work of the Evangelical Lutheran Church in Jordan and Palestine.

In 2002, Raheb moved to Vienna, Austria, where she works as an independent consultant on development cooperation and cross-cultural dialogue. She conducts lectures at various universities and teacher-training institutions in Austria and Germany, is a member of many committees on intercultural and interreligious dialogue, and has published various books and articles.

Adnan A. Musallam

Is Associate Professor of History at the Department of Humanities in Bethlehem University. He is a member of the administrative committee and Board of Trustees of al-Liqa' Center and ARIJ (Applied Research Institute-Jerusalem). He also serves on the ruling Board of the Good Shepherds School (Asooj). He has written many articles and books on Bethlehem and on Contemporary Islamic Thought.

Roberto Marin-Guzman

Obtained his Ph.D in Middle Eastern History and Islamic Studies from the University of Texas at Austin (1994). He also has two master's degrees in the same fields, one from El Colegio de Mexico in Mexico City, and the other from the University of Texas at Austin. He was Visiting Scholar at the University of Texas at Austin (2003) and at the American University in Cairo (2006-2007). Currently, he is a professor in History and Arabic Language at the University of Costa Rica.

Manzar Foroohar

Is a Professor of History at California Polytechnic State University, San Luis Obispo, California, where she has been teaching since 1987. Foroohar received her bachelor's degree in political science from National University, Tehran, Iran; her master's degree in political science from California State University, Northridge; and her doctorate in history from the University of California, Los Angeles. Her research and publications focus on the modern history of Latin America and the Middle East. Currently, she is working on the book *Palestinian Diaspora in Central America.*

Nicole Saffie Guevara

Was born in Santiago, Chile, in 1979. She is a third generation Palestinian who descends from a Catholic family from Bethlehem. She has a master's degree in Political Science and International Affairs from Pontificia Universidad Católica de Chile. Her focus is on international relations, migration, the Middle East, and the Palestinian-Israeli conflict. She writes about culture and politics for Al Damir magazine, which caters to the Palestinian community in Chile, and she participates in the Palestinian foundation "Bethlehem 2000",, which provides humanitarian assistance to the Palestinian people. She worked for two years on a project that encouraged dialogue between the Palestinian and Jewish youth of Chile – an initiative that was supported by the Ford Foundation. She has published papers on intercultural dialogue and migration, especially the Arab migrations to Chile (Revista Miscelánea de Estudios Árabes y Hebraicos, Sección Árabe – Islam, Vol. 54, 2005, Universidad de Granada).

Lorenzo Agar

Was born in Chile. His father was from one of the first Syrian families to emigrate to Chile. His mother came to Chile from Spain as a refugee of the civil war. He studied in France from 1974–1980 where he obtained his sociology degree in Latin America Studies (Diplôme D´Etudes Approfondies). He obtained a master's degree in Urban and Regional Development from the Catholic University of Chile. Since coming back to Chile, he has been conducting studies on international migration, especially the Arab migration to Chile. He has taught in several academic departments at the University of Chile. His research and publications focus on population, international migration, public health, research methods, urban development, and social policies. From 1995-2000 Agar was the Director of UNFPA/ECLAC/University of Chile´s International Program in Population and Sustainable Development. From 2006–2008 he was Coordinator of the Intercultural Dialogue between Arab and Jewish Community Youth in Chile, sponsored by the Ford Foundation. He was also an advisor for the Ministry of Health on immigrant and refugee health in Chile. Agar lectures at numerous conferences and international meetings, and he is currently the Director of the Refugees Department at the Vicar of the Social Pastoral in Chile and Professor at the Faculty of Medicine at the University of Chile.

Made in the USA
Lexington, KY
31 October 2013